KT-526-175

THE BEST OF
BROCHUREDESIGN8
WILLOUGHBY DESIGN GROUP

ROCKPORT

GLOUCESTER, MASSACHUSETTS

ROCKPORT
PUBLISHERS

THE BEST OF
BROCHUREDESIGN**8**
WILLOUGHBY DESIGN GROUP

© 2005 by Rockport Publishers, Inc.

All rights reserved. No part of this book
may be reproduced in any form without
written permission of the copyright owners.
All images in this book have been reproduced
with the knowledge and prior consent of
the artists concerned, and no responsibility
is accepted by producer, publisher, or
printer for any infringement of copyright
or otherwise, arising from the contents of
this publication. Every effort has been
made to ensure that credits accurately
comply with information supplied.

First published in the
United States of America by

Rockport Publishers, Inc.
33 Commercial Street
Gloucester, Massachusetts 01930-5089
Telephone: (978) 282-9590
Fax: (978) 283-2742

www.rockpub.com
ISBN 1-59253-121-0

10 9 8 7 6 5 4 3 2
Design: Willoughby Design Group
Printed in China

Park Library
University of Gloucestershire
Park Campus, The Park
Cheltenham
Gloucestershire
GL50 2RH

CONTE

008-035

CORPORATE

036-057

ANNUAL REPORTS

058-111

PRODUCTS | SERVICES

112-141

NONPROFIT | EDUCATIONAL
INSTITUTIONAL

142–197

SELF-PROMOTIONAL

198-219

ARTS | ENTERTAINMENT
EVENTS

220-223

DIRECTORY

224

ABOUT THE AUTHOR

INTRODUCTION

The basic purpose of a brochure is to make information understandable. Beyond effective communication, there are always other important objectives: creating desire, clarifying, selling, inspiring, educating, providing credibility, and building relationships. A brochure also speaks volumes about its moment in history. A brochure describes culture, place, technologies, economics, and the values and passions of designers and organizations that create artifacts worthy of remembering.

From nearly one thousand entries, we selected 183 brochures. The inclusions met six criteria for design excellence: overall impact, relevance, appropriateness (audience, message, context, use of materials), coherence, craftsmanship, and aesthetics.

Receiving hundreds of brochures each week, we assessed each entry based on its effectiveness as a communication tool. We sorted the entries into three levels: Exceptional, Superior, and Standard. After our initial screening, there were more than 300 brochures in the Exceptional category. With room for less than 200, our criteria for selection became critical.

Lacking access to companies' strategies and performance results, we based our final selections on all six criteria and celebrated additional qualities such as exceptional writing, use of humor, environmental responsibility, cultural impact, information handling, and experimental technologies.

Although the majority of entries were submitted in English, more than half of the brochures were submitted from outside the U.S. Entries came from a range of industries, including arts and entertainment, retail, nonprofit, promotional, and corporate.

It is obvious that the common thread running through the work is the designers' and clients' vision for quality and creativity. What is not shown in this book or articulated in sales figures is the designers' role in transforming abstract ideas and information into tangible and compelling experiences. The final selections for **The Best of Brochure Design 8** honor the designers and organizations that push beyond good to great.

We thank each of you for submitting inspiring brochures from every sector. It is good to see so much talent and such commitment to communication excellence.

Ann Willoughby and the Willoughby Design Team
Kansas City, Missouri

CORPORATE

EE+CHUNGDESIGNTHEDAVEANDALEXSHOWEATADVERTISINGDESIGNINCGRAFIKZDESIGN
BAUMAN
PENTAGRAMSFBURGARDDESIGNGROUP
MANNHANGER18CREATIVEGROUPHALLMARKLOYALTYEQUUSDESIGNCONSULTANTSPTELTD
BNIMARCHITECTSBBKSTUDIOHATTRICKDESIGN THEPOINTGROUP GEE+CHUNGDESIGNTHEDA
ALEXSHOW EATADVERTISING&DESIGNINC SALTERBAXTER BANDUJODONKER&BROT
AGRAMSFBURGARDDESIGNGROUPZUCCHINIDESIGNPTELTD HANGER18CREA
ROUP EQUUSDESIGNCONSULTANTSPTELTDBERTZDESIGNGROUP
IOTHEPOINTGROUPHATTRICKDESIGNGEE+CHUNGDESIGNTHEDAVEANDALEXSHOWEATADVERTISING
ICGRAFIKZDESIGNSALTERBAXTERBANDUJODONKER&BROTHERSPENTAGRAMDESIGNBURGARDDE
ROUPZUCCHINIDESIGNPTELTD HALLMARKLOYAL
ESIGNCONSULTANTSPTELTD BERTZDESIGNGROUPBNIMARCHITECTS THEPOINTGROUPH
GEE+CHUNGDESIGNTHEDAVEANDALEXSHOW GRAFIKZDESIGNSA
ER BANDUJODONKER&BROTHERS PENTAGRAMSFBURGARDDESIGNGROUPZUCCHINIDESIGNPTELTD
ANN&BAUMANNHANGER18CREATIVEGROUPHALLMARKLOYALTY
ERTZDESIGNGROUPBNIMARCHITECTSBBKSTUDIOTHEPOINTGROUP GFE+CHUNG
AVEANDALEXSHOWEATADVERTISING&DESIGNINC SALTERBAXTERBANDUJODONKE
PENTAGRAMSFBURGARDDESIGNGROUP BAUMANN&BAUMANNHAM
TIVEGROUPHALLMARKLOYALTYEQUUSDESIGNCONSULTANTSPTELTDBERTZDESIGNGROUPBNIMARC
KSTUDIOHATTRICKDESIGNTHEPOINTGROUP GEE+CHUNGDESIGN THEDAVEANDALEXSHOW EATADVE
IGNINCGRAFIKZDESIGN BANDUJODONKER&BROTHERSPENTAGRAMSFBURGARD
ROUPZUCCHINIDESIGNPTELTD BAUMANN&BAUMANNHANGER18CREATIVEGROUP
ESIGNCONSULTANTSPTELTD BNIMARCHITECTSBBKSTUDIOTHEPOINTGROUP
IGNGEE+CHUNGDESIGNTHEDAVEANDALEXSHOWEATADVERTISING&DESIGNINCGRAFIKZDESIGNSA
ER BANDUJODONKER&BROTHERSPENTAGRAMDESIGN BURGARDDESIGNGROUP ZUCCHINIDESIGNPT
ANN&BAUMANN HALLMARKLOYALTYEQUUSDESIGNCONSULTANTSPTEL
ERTZDESIGNGROUPBNIMARCHITECTSBBKSTUDIOTHEPOINTGROUP GEE+CHUNG
AVEANDALEXSHOW EATADVERTISING&DESIGNINCGRAFIKZDESIGNSALTERBAXTER BANDUJODO
AS BURGARDDESIGNGROUPZUCCHINIDESIGNPTELTDBAUMANN&BAUMANNHANGER
TIVEGROUPHALLMARKLOYALTY PTELTDBERTZDESIGNGROUPBNIMA
KSTUDIOTHEPOINTGROUPHATTRICKDESIGNGEE+CHUNGDESIGNTHEDAVEANDALEXSHOW
GNINGRAFIKZDESIGNSALTERBAXTER PENTAGRAMSFBURGARDDES
ROUPZUCCHINIDESIGNPTELTDBAUMANN&BAUMANNHANGER18CREATIVEGROUPHALLMARKLOYA

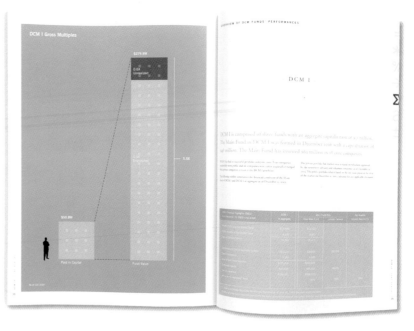

GEE + CHUNG DESIGN
DCM IV Offering Memorandum

ART DIRECTOR:	DESIGNERS:	CLIENT:	TOOLS:	MATERIALS:
Earl Gee	Earl Gee	DCM—Doll Capital	Adobe Photoshop	Stora Enso Centura Dull
	Fani Chung	Management	Adobe InDesign	100 lb (text)

010

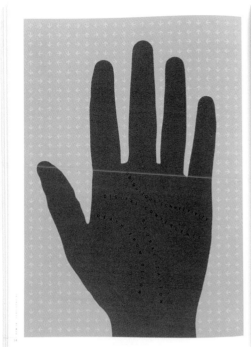

THE DAVE AND ALEX SHOW

Modem Media View Book

ART DIRECTORS:	DESIGNER:	CLIENT:	TOOLS:	MATERIALS:
Alexander Isley	Tracie Rosenkopf-	Modem Media	QuarkXPress	Monadnock
Dave Goldenber	Lissauer			

EAT ADVERTISING & DESIGN, INC.

Capabilities Brochure/Engineering Firm

ART DIRECTOR:	DESIGNER:	CLIENT:	TOOLS:	MATERIALS:
Patrice Eilts-Jobe	John Storey	SK Design	Adobe Photoshop	Pacesetter
John Storey			Adobe Illustrator	
			QuarkXPress	

GRAFIKZ DESIGN
Target

ART DIRECTOR:
Andrei Polessi

CLIENT:
Target Engenharia

TOOLS:
Adobe Illustrator

SALTERBAXTER

Boodle Hatfield Corporate Brochure

ART DIRECTOR:	DESIGNER:	CLIENT:	TOOLS:	MATERIALS:
Alan Delgado	Alan Delgado	Boodle Hatfield	QuarkXPress	Rives Reflections (cover)
				Robert Horne Natural (text)

BANDUJO DONKER & BROTHERS

Citigroup Private Bank—Investment Expertise

ART DIRECTOR:	DESIGNER:	CLIENT:	TOOLS:	MATERIALS:
Bob Brothers	Laura Astuto	Citigroup Private Bank	Adobe Photoshop QuarkXPress	Mohawk Navajo

BANDUJO DONKER & BROTHERS

Citigroup Private Bank—The Tailored Group

ART DIRECTOR:	DESIGNER:	CLIENT:	TOOLS:	MATERIALS:
Bob Brothers	Laura Astuto	Citigroup Private Bank	Adobe Photoshop QuarkXPress	Mohawk Navajo

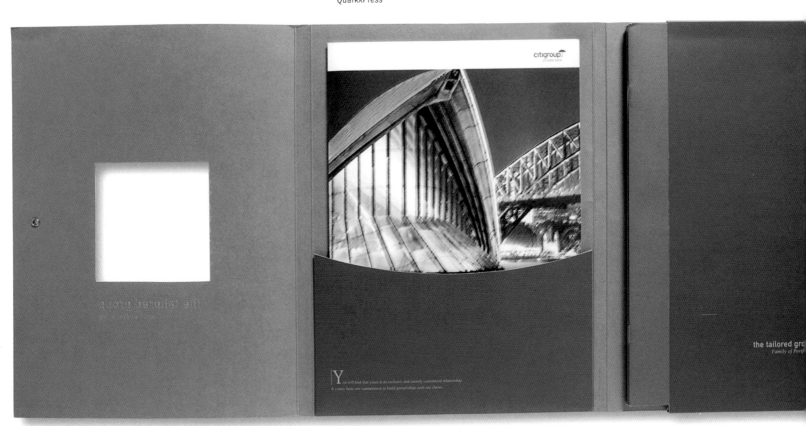

PENTAGRAM DESIGN/SF
Sales Brochure

ART DIRECTOR:	DESIGNER:	CLIENT:	TOOLS:
Kit Hinrichs	Laura Scott	Muzak	Adobe Photoshop
			Adobe Illustrator
			QuarkXPress

ART DIRECTOR:	DESIGNER:	CLIENT:	TOOLS:	MATERIALS:
Todd Burgard	Todd Burgard	ADG Marketing Communications	QuarkXPress	Productolith dull two-color match and varnish

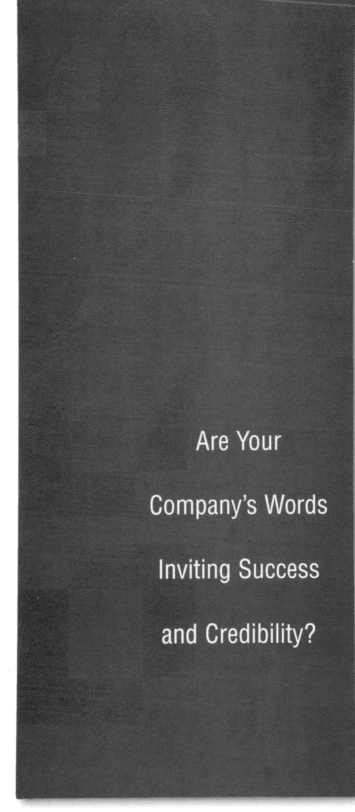

Are Your

Company's Words

Inviting Success

and Credibility?

[MORE OR LESS IS NOT GOOD ENOUGH]

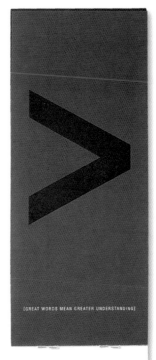

[GREAT WORDS MEAN GREATER UNDERSTANDING]

IS YOUR MESSAGE CLEAR?

Your business's marketing message must be effectively broadcast in every booklet, advertisement, annual report, sales piece, brochure, business card, handout, white paper, newsletter, Web site, and press release. United and cohesive. Your logo, tag line, and brand identity should be explicit and memorable.

When I sent one of our own marketing pieces to potential clients, a follow-up phone call produced the words every business owner wants to hear: "Anne, I have your Ten Tips article on my desk, and I refer to it often. We need to talk."

Top-of-mind awareness is critical to business success. It's imperative that your customers think of you first when they need the type of service you provide.

Will they know who you are and how to reach you? If not, *Anne Dieter Gallaher Marketing Communications* can help increase your visibility and credibility by producing the finest professional marketing pieces appropriate for your industry niche.

5 MARKETING BENCHMARKS TO TEST YOUR COMMUNICATIONS SUCCESS

1. Based on your printed sales and marketing pieces, would you buy your product or service? Is your brochure attractive, inviting, beneficial, and errorless?
2. If you were the customer, would you save your communications pieces? Is there great stuff in your brochure that clients will want to keep and refer to? Or does it look like the piece was written and produced for next to nothing? If so, your sales results probably indicate you received "next to nothing."
3. If you're the best, the expert, the safest, the most accomplished, do your company's pieces broadcast that message? Captivate customers with why they need you, and do it at least seven times a year.
4. Do you know what your competition is producing? Although you may be the best service provider, perhaps your competition is marketing itself better and more aggressively.
5. Are your current marketing pieces successful and on budget? Well-written words inform, educate, sell, and increase a company's bottom line. A business needs to remain visible and constantly project its value; otherwise, Company B will consume its market share.

If you answered No to any of these 5 Marketing Benchmarks, call us for fresh ideas on how to capture your best message and proclaim it in the marketplace.

019

CORPORATE

The Brand

EVOKE

The Evoke brand characteristics
How do people outside the company
describe us? How do we describe ourselves?
Those descriptions, or characteristics,
comprise our corporate personality. And
much like human personality, it leaves
a lasting impression. What's more, our
personality distinguishes us from our
competitors. All of our professional efforts
should be compatible with the following
brand characteristics:

Exclusive

Experienced

Passionate

Driven

Committed

Reputable

Where we've been. Where we're headed.
Evoke software solves real and profound
problems. Our growth is aligned with
the rapid expansion of corporate data worldwide. Our market is huge and is getting
bigger. So are we.

PENTAGRAM DESIGN/SF
Brand Standards Manual

ART DIRECTOR:	**DESIGNER:**	**CLIENT:**	**TOOLS:**
Kit Hinrichs	Leslie Stitzlein	Evoke Software Co.	Adobe Photoshop
			Adobe Illustrator
			QuarkXPress

Creating a powerful brand.
Disney. FedEx. McDonald's. Hewlett-Packard. IBM. Microsoft.
Mention the world's strongest brand names and we immediately conjure mental snapshots of what those brands
represent. That mental snapshot is brand image, the
cumulative impression a company makes on the public.

And brand image, for the most part, grows out of brand
identity, which is the sum of all the outward manifestations
of the brand. These tangible characteristics range from our

products and services, our name, logo, typeface, packag-
ing and website all the way to the manner in which we
answer the phone.

Keeping the Evoke brand strong requires that all the
tangible elements of our brand identity must be surrounded
by the halo of our brand values and characteristics—the
way we operate when nobody's watching. And the more we
live the principles of our brand values, the more naturally
our brand identity will come to represent them.

B®and

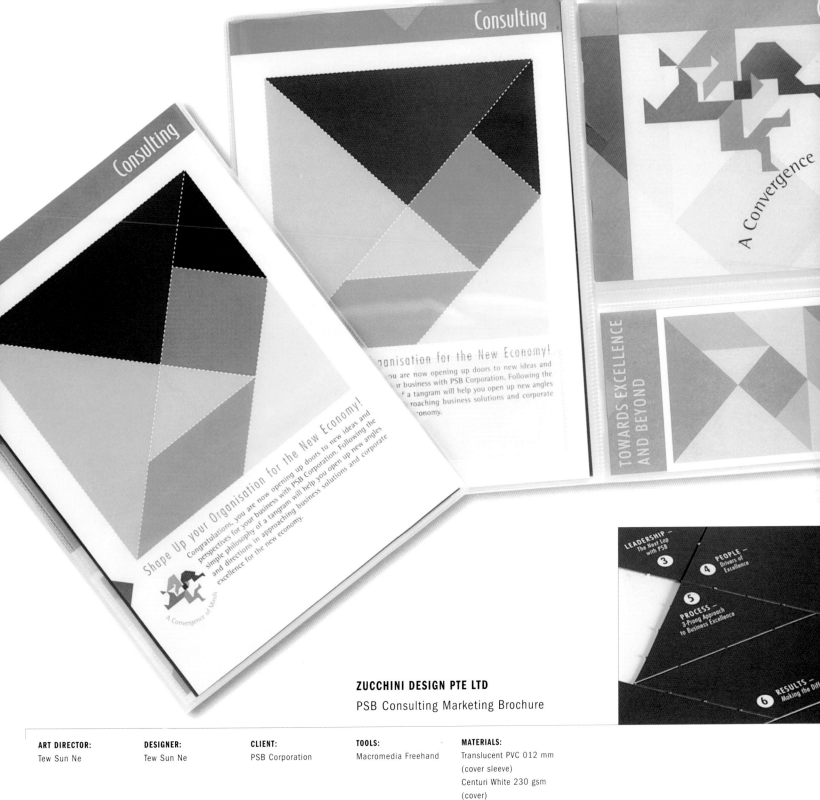

ZUCCHINI DESIGN PTE LTD

PSB Consulting Marketing Brochure

ART DIRECTOR:	DESIGNER:	CLIENT:	TOOLS:	MATERIALS:
Tew Sun Ne	Tew Sun Ne	PSB Corporation	Macromedia Freehand	Translucent PVC 012 mm (cover sleeve) Centuri White 230 gsm (cover) Aspire 130 gsm (text)

021

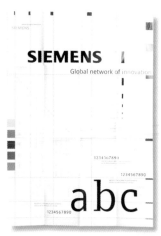
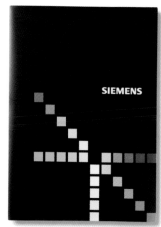
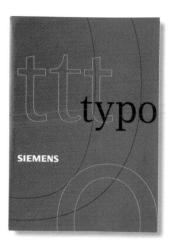

BAUMANN & BAUMANN
Siemens Brand Elements

ART DIRECTORS:
Barbara and Gerd
Baumann

DESIGNERS:
Barbara and Gerd
Baumann

CLIENT:
Siemens AG
Corporate
Communications

TOOLS:
Adobe InDesign
Adobe Photoshop
Macromedia Freehand

MATERIALS:
Phoenix Motion

022

So you see, at Econotech Services, we are experts in seeing what others don't. Specifically in the areas of pulping, bleaching, pulp and paper testing, microscopy & wood technology, process chemical analyses and environmental analyses. And since the company was formed in 1972, we've grown to be one of the largest independent pulp and paper testing laboratories in the world.

Accurate, rapid and reliable results are key to our company's substantial expansion, as is the recognized knowledge of our staff. Our initial team of 11 experts has grown to include over 30 research professionals with expertise in chip testing, pulping, bleaching, pulp and paper testing, dissolving pulp evaluation, microscopy, environmental analysis and testing of process samples and liquors. Within a single 19,000 square foot facility, Econotech can perform over 400 analytical tests on everything from wood to finished product, around 100 tests on pulp and paper products and over 50 different microscopy tests.

Econotech's international clientele includes pulp and paper mills, equipment suppliers, chemical suppliers, consulting engineers and universities. In addition to providing unbiased, independent and confidential evaluations of new processes or chemicals, Econotech assists clients in the development of new equipment, the design of new mills and the evaluation of chemical costs involved in mill modernization. >>

HANGAR 18 CREATIVE GROUP
Econotech Brochure

DESIGNER:
Kim Wolf

CLIENT:
Econotech Services

TOOLS:
QuarkXPress

MATERIALS:
Cougar Opaque
(text and cover)

Microscopy is an indispensable testing discipline for the pulp and paper industry. The primary application is fiber analysis, which provides detailed evaluations of wood species and pulp type in paper, pulp and wood samples.

Contaminant identification is also a large portion of the work we do in the Microscopy Department. This provides valuable assistance in process troubleshooting. In addition to light microscopic techniques, we have access to scanning electron microscopy and Fourier Transform infra red analysis. Digital photomicrographs enhance reports and provide instant visualization of contaminants and defects.

Microscopy is an art as much as a science and requires many years of training and experience to become proficient. The Microscopy Group has over 30 years combined experience in analyzing the untold variety of samples that are submitted. We have extensive reference resources including natural and man made fibers, particle and contaminant samples and permanent slides. >>

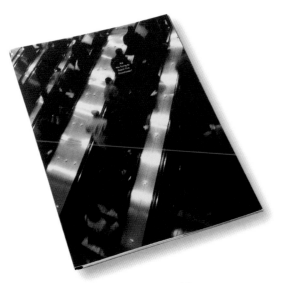

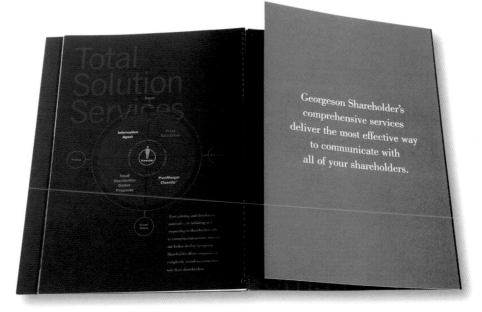

PENTAGRAM DESIGN/SF

Corporate Communications

ART DIRECTOR:
Kit Hinrichs

DESIGNER:
David Asari

CLIENT:
Georgeson Sharehold

TOOLS:
Adobe Photoshop
Adobe Illustrator
QuarkXPress

025

alternative investments
The Basics and Beyond

THE CITIGROUP
PRIVATE BANK

*Alternative investments' historically low correlation
with traditional investments is crucial.*

Benefits of Diversification

Figure A. Correlation of Alternative & Traditional Asset Classes

	Hedge Funds	Private Equity	U.S. Equity	U.S. Bonds	World Equity	World Bonds	Real Estate	Credit Structures
Hedge Funds	1.00	0.72	0.55	(0.16)	0.57	(0.34)	(0.20)	0.21
Private Equity		1.00	0.64	(0.28)	0.64	(0.25)	0.06	0.17
U.S. Equity			1.00	(0.08)	0.82	(0.07)	0.13	0.27
U.S. Bonds				1.00	(0.15)	0.70	0.06	(0.18)
World Equity					1.00	0.01	0.09	0.26
World Bonds						1.00	(0.02)	0.13
Real Estate							1.00	(0.15)
Credit Structures								1.00

BANDUJO DONKER & BROTHERS

Citigroup Private Bank—Alternative Investments

ART DIRECTOR:
Bob Brothers

DESIGNER:
Laura Astuto

CLIENT:
Citigroup Private Bank

TOOLS:
Adobe Photoshop
QuarkXPress

MATERIALS:
Mohawk Navajo

*Major categories of alternative investments include
hedge funds, private equity and real estate.*

A Variety of Alternative Investments

HALLMARK LOYALTY

How to Stand Out in the Crowd: Profiting from Personalization

ART DIRECTOR:
Christopher Huelshorst

DESIGNER:
Christine Taylor

EDITORIAL DIRECTOR:
Stacey Hsu

COPYWRITER:
Janet Walnik

PHOTOGRAPHY:
Ambrosi & Associates,
Chicago

PRINTER:
Nies Artcraft, St. Louis

CLIENT:
State Farm

TOOLS:
QuarkXPress

MATERIALS:
Mohawk Superfine

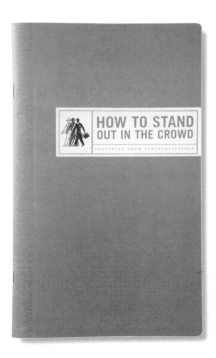

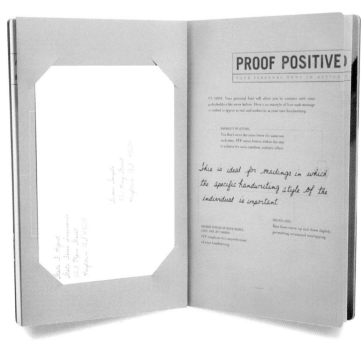

027

CORPORATE

EQUUS DESIGN CONSULTANTS PTE LTD
Corporate Brochure

ART DIRECTOR:	DESIGNERS:	CLIENT:	TOOLS:	MATERIALS:
Andrew Thomas	Tay Chin Thiam	Raffles International	Adobe Photoshop	Woodfree
	Andrew Thomas		QuarkXPress	

swissôtel **UNLOCKED**

In Australia, Asia, Europe or the Americas, our hotels are located downtown in proximity to the airport, the business district, shopping, entertainment and all forms of transportation. Contemporary design is combined with local flavour to give each hotel a distinctive character.

ALL THE ROOMS REFLECT OUR HALLMARK ATTENTION TO DETAIL, WITH EACH FULLY EQUIPPED FOR YOUR BUSINESS NEEDS, WHATEVER THEY MAY BE.

BERTZ DESIGN GROUP
Bausch & Lomb 150th Anniversary Book

ART DIRECTOR:
Andrew Wessels

DESIGNER:
Andrew Wessels

CLIENT:
Bausch & Lomb

TOOLS:
Adobe Photoshop
QuarkXPress

MATERIALS:
Sedona black leather
(cover)
Appleton Utopia 1X
Bright White 100 lb
(text)

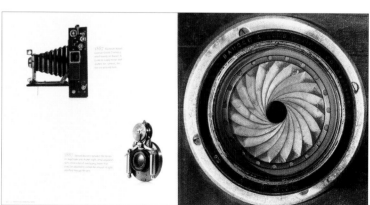

BNIM ARCHITECTS

Los Angeles County Natural History Museum

ART DIRECTOR:
Zack Shubkagel

DESIGNER:
Erin Gehle

CLIENT:
Los Angeles County
Natural History Museum

TOOLS:
Adobe InDesign
Adobe Illustrator

MATERIALS:
8 x 11 vellum wrapped
(cover) with sticky back
vellum (cover) and
pages

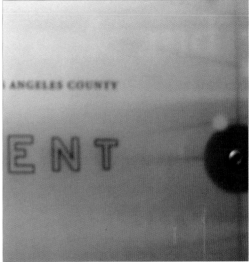

BBK STUDIO

HMI Dealer Merchandising Program

ART DIRECTOR:	DESIGNER:	CLIENT:	TOOLS:	MATERIALS:
Sharon Oleniczak	Brian Hauch	Herman Miller	QuarkXPress	Carnival Pure White 80 lb C Smooth

THE POINT GROUP
Marketing Services Sales Brochure

ART DIRECTOR:	DESIGNER:	CLIENT:	TOOLS:	MATERIALS:
David Howard	Crethann Hickman	MARC	QuarkXPress	Mohawk Navajo

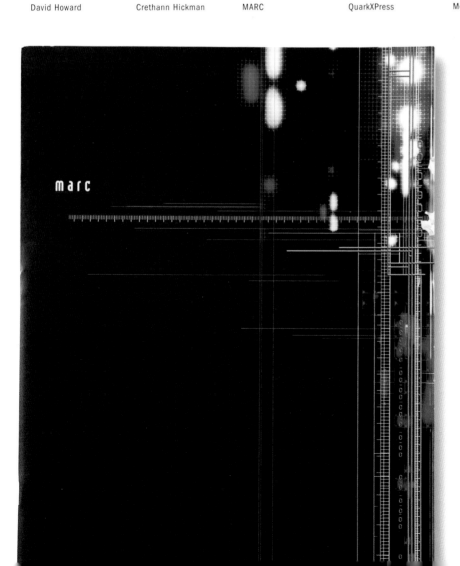

HAT-TRICK DESIGN

30 Gresham Street

ART DIRECTORS:
Gareth Howat
David Kimpton
Jim Sutherland

DESIGNERS:
Gareth Howat
David Kimpton
Jim Sutherland
Adam Giles

CLIENT:
Land Securities

TOOLS:
Adobe Photoshop
Adobe Illustrator
QuarkXPress

MATERIALS:
Millenium Gloss
Neptune Unique
Colourplan

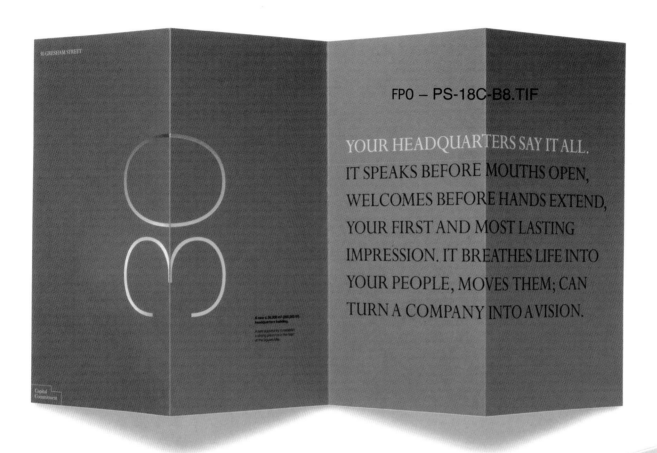

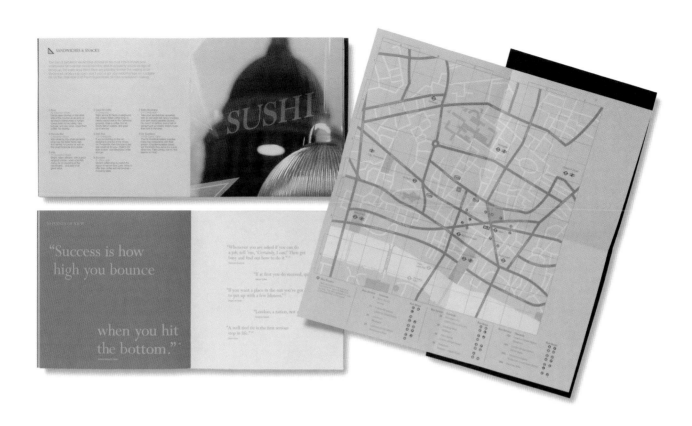

SALTERBAXTERRIONDONDESIGN CARBONESMOLANAGENCYHOWRYDESIGNASSOCIATESWEY
OUTHDESIGNPERKSDESIGNPARTNERS IMELDAAGENCYPOPCORNINITIATIVEHORNALLAND
DESIGNWORKSINC SALTERBAXTERRIONDONDESIGNGRAFIKZCARBONESMOLANAGENCY HOWRYD
ASSOCIATES WEYMOUTHDESIGNPERKSDESIGNPARTNERSMONSTER POPCORNINITIA
ORNALLANDERSONDESIGNWORKSINCSALTERBAXTER GRAFIKZ
HOWRYDESIGNASSOCIATESWEYMOUTHDESIGN PERKSDESIGNPARTNERS MONSTERIMELDAAGENCY
PCORNINITIATIVEHORNALLANDERSONDESIGNWORKSINC RIONDONDESIGNGRAFIKZ
ARBONESMOLANAGENCY HOWRYDESIGNASSOCIATESWEYMOUTHDESIGN
IMELDAAGENCY HORNALLANDERSONDESIGNWORKSINCSALTERBAXTER
DESIGN GRAFIKZ CARBONE HOWRYDESIGNASSOCIATESWEYMOUTHDESIGN
MONSTERIMELDAAGENCYPOPCORNINITIATIVEHORNALLANDERSONDESIGNWORKSIN
LTERBAXTERRIONDONDESIGNGRAFIKZCARBONESMOLANAGENCYHOWRYDESIGNASSOCIATESWEY
OUTHDESIGNPERKSDESIGNPARTNERSMONSTER POPCORNINITIATIVEHORNALLAND
SALTERBAXTERRIONDONDESIGNGRAFI CARBONESMOLANAGENCYHOWRYD
ASSOCIATESWEYMOUTHDESIGN MONSTERIMELDAAGENCY
ORNALLANDERSONDESIGNWORKSINC SALTERBAXTERRIONDONDESIGNGRAFIKZ
HOWRYDESIGNASSOCIATES WEYMOUTHDESIGNPERKSDESIGNPARTNERS IMELDAAGENCY
OPCORNINITIATIVE HORNALLANDERSONDESIGNWORKSINC SALTERBAXTERRIONDONDESIG
ARBONESMOLANAGENCYHOWRYDESIGNASSOCIATESW PERKSDESIGNPARTNERS
IMELDAAGENCYPOPCORNINITIATIVEHORNALLANDERSONDESIGNWORKSINC RIO
ONDESIGNGRAFIKZCARBONESMOLANAGENCYHOWRYDESIGNASSOCIATESWEYMOUTHDESIGNPERK
GNPARTNERSMONSTER POPCORNINITIATIVEHORNALLANDERSONDESIGNWORKSIN
LTERBAXTERRIONDONDESIGNGRAFIKZ HOWRYDESIGNASSOCIATESWEY
OUTHDESIGNPERKSDESIGNPARTNERSMONSTER IMELDAAGENCYPOPCORNINITIATIVEHORNALLAND
ONDESIGNWORKSINC RIONDONDESIGN GRAFIKZCARBONESMOLANAGENCYHOWRY
ASSOCIATESWEYMOUTHDESIGNPERKSDESIGNPARTNERS IMELDAAGENCYPOPCORNINITIA
ORNALLANDERSONDESIGNWORKSINCSALTERBAXTER RIONDONDESIGN CARBONESMOLANA
MONSTERIMELDAAGEN

DIRECTIONS#3
TRENDS IN CSR REPORTING 2002-03
A JOINT REPORT BY SALTERBAXTER & CONTEXT
context salterbaxter

038

132 companies reports on environmental performance
100 companies report on social and ethical performance

118
companies are defined as non-reporters

Software and Computer Services has reporters
Support Services has the most first-time reporters:
Personal Care & Household Products, Tobacco and Utilities all have
reporting

45 companies have independent verification

29 companies reported for the first time this year

56
companies produce no information of substance

SALTERBAXTER

Directions 3 Report

ART DIRECTOR:	DESIGNER:	CLIENT:	TOOLS:	MATERIALS:
Alan Delgado	Alan Delgado	Salterbaxter	QuarkXPress	Flockage cover

Never put a bunny on the cover!

The birth rate began to grow in 2001 with a fast increasing number of companies producing CSR reports. We asked in Directions 2 if the growth was sustainable and whether the business case was compelling enough to keep companies reporting.

Our research shows the answer is a definite yes. The combined pressures of corporate governance reform, the threat of legislation in Europe and the UK, and the activities of the socially responsible investment community, are driving ever more companies to report on ever more issues.

Find the key figures and analysis on page 13, and a detailed breakdown by sector on page 20.

For over a decade UK governments have consistently championed environmental and social reporting, and deserve credit for the relatively high level of participation among UK companies. On page 2, s ord Whitty the UK's Environment and Business Minister argues greater disclosure is good for business. Max Tyrrel of HSBC reviews the influence of socially responsible investment (SRI) (page 4) and hopes the issues will become so mainstream that the SRI community will return to oblivion.

We also point to the growing importance of internal CSR communications and peer at the horizon to find the next hot issues for companies to manage. And for those about to write their first CSR report, we offer some tips to enhance clarity and build credibility.

As ever, your feedback is most welcome.

WEYMOUTH DESIGN

Sappi 2002 Annual Report Show

ART DIRECTOR:	DESIGNERS:	CLIENT:	TOOLS:	MATERIALS:
Tom Laidlaw	Robert Krivicich	Sappi Fine Paper	QuarkXPress	Sappi Fine Paper
	Brad Lewthwaite	North America	Adobe Photoshop	

ANNUAL REVIEW 2003

The art of bringing the right people together

EU ERNST & YOUNG
Quality In Everything We Do

SALTERBAXTER

Ernst & Young Annual Review 2003

DESIGNER:	CLIENT:	TOOLS:	MATERIALS:	MATERIALS:
Mark Pailing	Ernst & Young	QuarkXPress	Naturalis Arctic White smooth 250 gsm (cover)	Naturalis Arctic White smooth 135 gsm (text)

041

ANNUAL REPORTS

B R A S I L P A R

GRAFIKZ
Brasilpar

ART DIRECTOR:
Andrei Polessi

CLIENT:
Brasilpar

TOOLS:
Adobe Illustrator
QuarkXPress

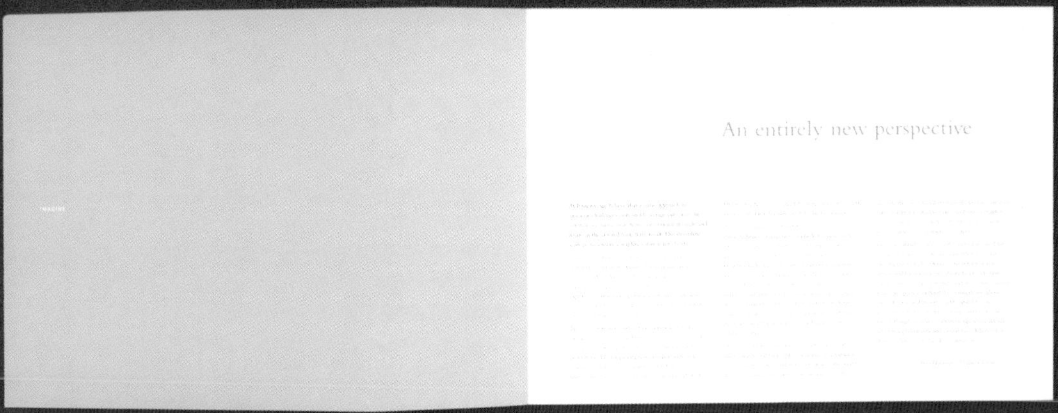

An entirely new perspective

Reflection brings clarity

CARBONE SMOLAN AGENCY
Imagine

ART DIRECTOR:
Justin Peters

CLIENT:
Imagine Reinsurance

MATERIALS:
Wausau's Astrobright

An Alternate Perspective
THE IMAGINE GROUP VOLUME ONE

The time
is now

HOWRY DESIGN ASSOCIATES

Xoma 2003 Annual Report

ART DIRECTOR:	DESIGNER:	CLIENT:	TOOLS:	MATERIALS:
Jill Howry	Ty Whittington	Xoma	Adobe Photoshop QuarkXPress	Mohawk Superfine Strathmore Opaque

044

THE BEST OF
BROCHURE DESIGN 8

SEX
HAS BEEN PROVEN TO BE GOOD
FOR YOUR HEALTH.

VIVUS 03

HOWRY DESIGN ASSOCIATES

Viuus 2003 Annual Report

ART DIRECTOR:	DESIGNER:	CLIENT:	TOOLS:	MATERIALS:
Jill Howry	Ty Whittington	Vivus Inc	Adobe Photoshop QuarkXPress	Utopia II matte 80 lb

ED
(ERECTILE DYSFUNCTION)
IS THE INABILITY TO ACHIEVE OR
SUSTAIN AN ERECTION ADEQUATE
FOR SATISFYING SEXUAL ACTIVITY.

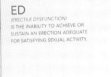

045

Work

Team

WEYMOUTH DESIGN

Millipore AR 2003

ART DIRECTOR:	DESIGNER:	WRITER:	PHOTOGRAPHER:	TOOLS:	MATERIALS:
Michael Weymouth	Bob Kellerman	Tom Anderson	Michael Weymouth	Adobe Photoshop Adobe Illustrator QuarkXPress	100 lb Sappi McCoy matte (cover) 100 lb Sappi McCoy matte (text)

046

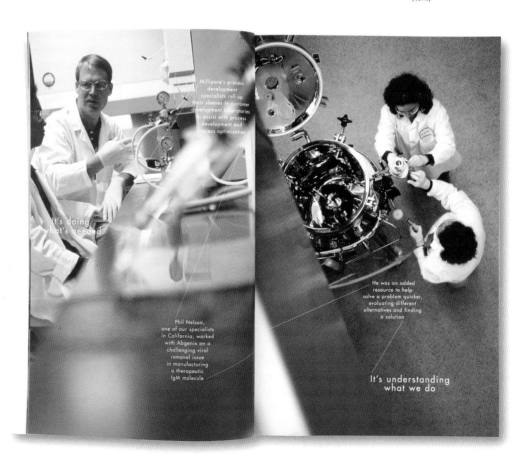

moving forward

PERKS DESIGN PARTNERS

Australian Pacific Airports Corporation, Annual Report 2003

ART DIRECTOR:	DESIGNER:	CLIENT:	TOOLS:	MATERIALS:
Chris Perks	Reina Alessio	Australia Pacific Airports Corporation	QuarkXPress	Navajo

SALTERBAXTER

B Sky B Annual Report 2003

ART DIRECTOR:	DESIGNER:	CLIENT:	TOOLS:	MATERIALS:
Penny Baxter	Ivan Angell	B Sky B Group PLC	QuarkXPress	Hello Silk 170 gsm (text)
				Hi Speed Popset Mist
				120 gsm (text)
				270 Color Plan (cover), wire

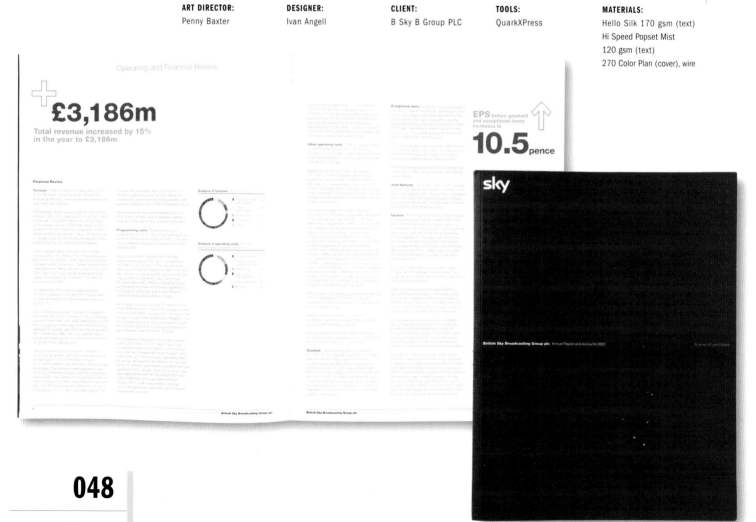

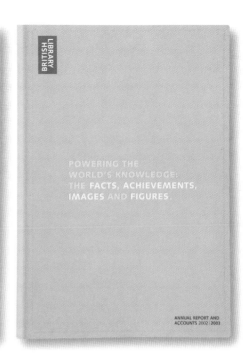

SALTERBAXTER

British Library Annual Report 2002-2003

ART DIRECTOR:	DESIGNER:	CLIENT:	TOOLS:	MATERIALS:
Penny Baxter	Hannah Griffiths	British Library	QuarkXPress	Hello Silk 150 gsm (text) Arjo Wiggins "Impressions Design" 300 gsm (cover)

28 years
It would take you **28 years**, day and night, to listen to the Sound Archive's entire CD collection.

Our basement stores reach **24 metres** below ground
– the equivalent of an **8** storey building, and as deep as the Victoria line which runs through them.

599km
Our collection fills **599** kilometres of shelving on **5** sites in London and Yorkshire.

We hold information on **25** different materials, including glass, bone, wood, stone, papyrus, plastic, wax, skin, bark, cloth, paper, metal and clay.

17,800
St Pancras Reading Rooms are open **6** days a week and every day Readers consult an average of **17,800** items.

The world's first Sunday paper, The Observer, is **212** years old. We have the **4** page first issue; copies now have **194** pages, and on the CD-Rom version every word can be searched.

8,490,04U
8,490,040 searches were made of our catalogue on the web during the year.

MONSTER DESIGN

Unitus Annual Report

ART DIRECTORS:
Theresa Monica
Hannah Wygal

DESIGNER:
Madeleine Eiche

CLIENT:
Unitus

TOOLS:
Adobe Photoshop
Macromedia Freehand
QuarkXPress

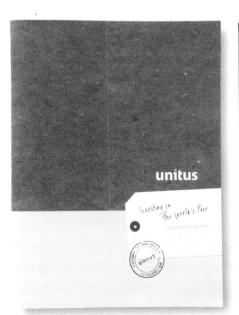

050

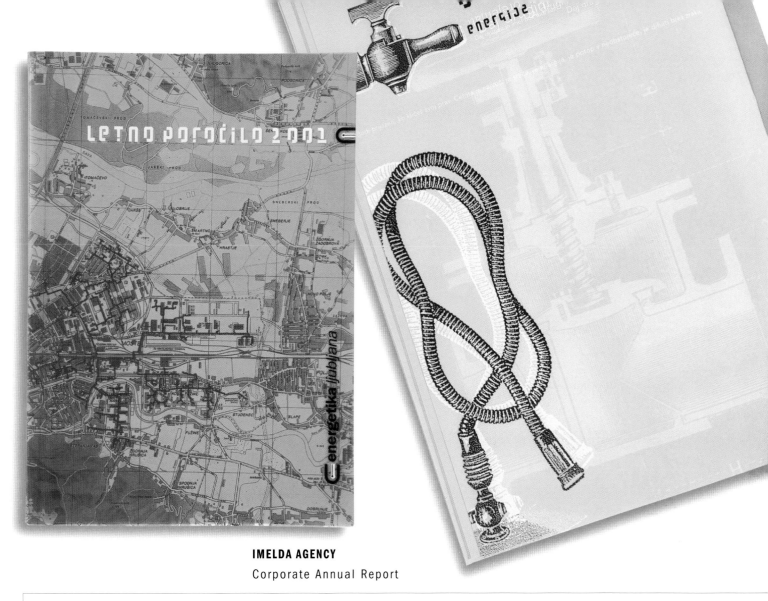

IMELDA AGENCY

Corporate Annual Report

Art Director:	Designer:	Client:	Materials:
Urukalo Saso	Urukalo Saso	Energetika Ljublyana	on offset

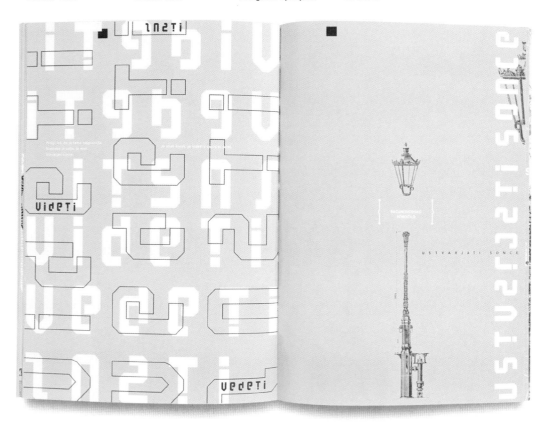

051

POPCORN INITIATIVE
KUA 2003 Annual Report: ON

ART DIRECTOR:
Chris Jones

DESIGNERS:
Chris Jones
Roger Wood

CLIENT:
Client (Gent. Kissimmee
Utility Authority

TOOLS:
Adobe InDesign
Adobe Illustrator

MATERIALS:
Fox River
Coronado SST
Stipple 80 lb (cover)
formed rubber

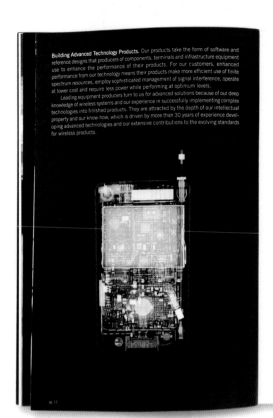

Building Advanced Technology Products. Our products take the form of software and reference designs that producers of components, terminals and infrastructure equipment use to enhance the performance of their products. For our customers, enhanced performance from our technology means their products make more efficient use of finite spectrum resources, employ sophisticated management of signal interference, operate at lower cost and require less power while performing at optimum levels.

Leading equipment producers turn to us for advanced solutions because of our deep knowledge of wireless systems and our experience in successfully implementing complex technologies into finished products. They are attracted by the depth of our intellectual property and our know-how, which is driven by more than 30 years of experience developing advanced technologies and our extensive contributions to the evolving standards for wireless products.

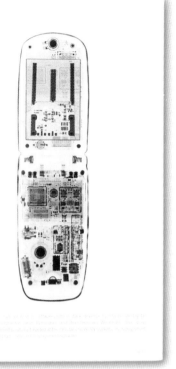

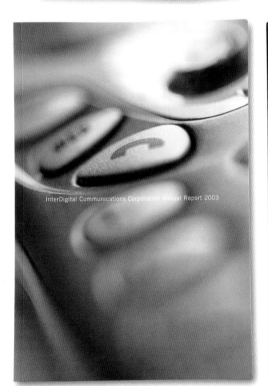

InterDigital Communications Corporation Annual Report 2003

Developing Technology. We create value through our sustained investment in core technology development and the adaptation of that technology for use in a broad array of product applications. Over the course of our history, we have designed and developed a wide range of technologies that form the basis for the vast majority of wireless communications around the world today and in the future. We patent many of our inventions and license those inventions to wireless communications equipment producers and related suppliers. We are constantly working toward the next breakthrough in wireless communications to bring to equipment producers, and ultimately consumers of their products, more wireless communications capability at lower costs.

Conceptualization. Start with a concept. Have a vision of a solution to a problem that does not yet exist. We began developing the constructs for a commercial digital mobile system in the 1980s, years before the products containing those inventions became widely available. In the early 1990s, we envisioned a system that would deliver broadband digital wireless voice and data. That system, incorporating our technology, is now becoming a reality as 3G wireless networks are turned on around the world.

WEYMOUTH DESIGN
InterDigital 2003 Annual Report

ART DIRECTOR:
Tom Laidlaw

DESIGNERS:
Arvi Raquel-Santos
Brad Lewthwaite

CLIENT:
InterDigital
Communications
Corporation

TOOLS:
Adobe Illustrator
QuarkXPress

MATERIALS:
Sappi McCoy Silk

053

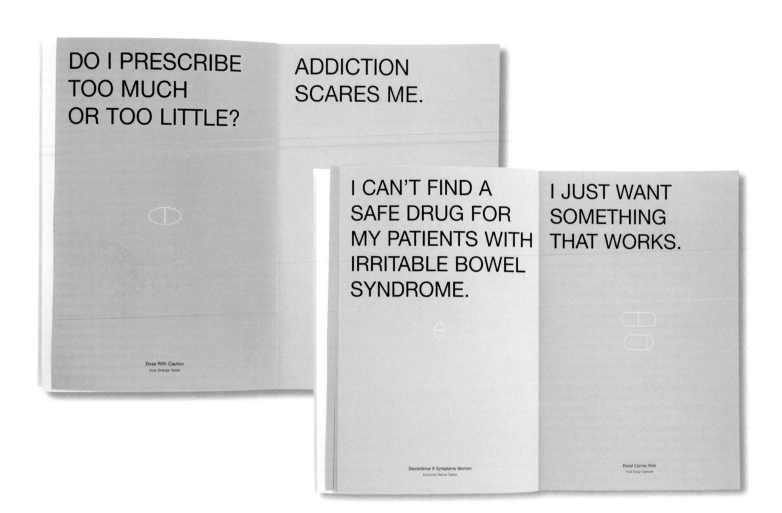

DO I PRESCRIBE TOO MUCH OR TOO LITTLE?

ADDICTION SCARES ME.

I CAN'T FIND A SAFE DRUG FOR MY PATIENTS WITH IRRITABLE BOWEL SYNDROME.

I JUST WANT SOMETHING THAT WORKS.

Dose With Caution
Oval Orange Tablet

Discontinue If Symptoms Worsen
Diamond Yellow Tablet

Relief Carries Risk
Oval Gray Capsule

HOWRY DESIGN ASSOCIATES

Pain Therapeutics 2003 Annual Report

ART DIRECTOR:	DESIGNER:	CLIENT:	TOOLS:	MATERIALS:
Jill Howry	Todd Richards	Pain Therapeutics	Adobe Photoshop QuarkXPress	McCoy Silk 100 lb, 130 lb

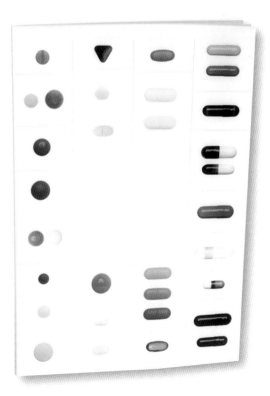

HORNALL ANDERSON DESIGN WORKS, INC.

Tree Top 2003 Annual Report

ART DIRECTOR:	DESIGNERS:	CLIENT:	TOOLS:	MATERIALS:
Katha Dalton	Katha Dalton	Tree Top	Adobe Photoshop	Mohawk 100 lb
	Tiffany Place		QuarkXPress	Superfine Text Smooth
	John Anderle			Ultrawhite (text)
	Beckon Wyld			Mohawk 80 lb Superfine
				Text Smooth Ultrawhite
				(inserts)
				Mohawk 100 lb
				Superfine Cover Smooth
				Ultrawhite (cover)

WEYMOUTH DESIGN

Courier 2003 Annual Report

ART DIRECTOR:	**DESIGNER:**	**CLIENT:**	**TOOLS:**	**MATERIALS:**
Robert Krivicich	Aaron Haesaert	Courier Corporation	Adobe Photoshop Adobe Illustrator QuarkXPress	Sappi McCoy, Finch Opaque

pay attention
to shareholders

$2.5M

PRODUCTS | SERVICES

STRETCHING THE BOUND

VERSATILE

At Colourscan, our philosophy has alw

customer's needs, and invest in whatever

capabilities will help us to serve them bet

we already dominate the market in pre-p

capabilities to cover press and post-press

words, the complete hat trick. And what

logy, you can be sure we have invested in t

high-end drum scanners and the ver

technologies, to Heidelberg presses and fu

it all, we can receive any client format ava

artwork to broadband file transmissio

(CTP) technologies.

9

EQUUS DESIGN CONSULTANTS PTE LTD

Brochure

ART DIRECTOR:	DESIGNERS:	CLIENT:	TOOLS:	MATERIALS:
Andrew Thomas	Andrew Thomas Gan Meng Teng	Colourscan Co. Pte Ltd	Adobe Photoshop Adobe Illustrator QuarkXPress	Maple Snow

In our continuing pursuit of excellence in reproduction, Colourscan have always made it a policy to employ the best tools for the job. Just as we've built our global reputation on our craft skills, so we also keep abreast of each new advance in modern technology, and set the pace by continually upgrading our resources with the most cutting-edge software and hardware. From origination to print production to finishing, we aim to ensure that our equipment and facilities truly push the boundaries.

n to anticipate our
ology, equipment or
t's why even though
e have extended our
s as well – in other
e service or techno-
best available, from
st digital imaging
ng facilities. To top
from traditional flat
Computer-to-Plate

IN OUR
FACILITIES

IN OUR
WOR

IN OUR
CAPABILITIE

061

VINTNERS INN
BY FERRARI-CARANO

Centrally located in Sonoma County, just 60 miles north of San Francisco, Vintners Inn is uniquely designed to make your stay – brief or extended, business or personal – a truly first class experience.

VINTNERS INN

JOHN ASH & CO

BY FERRARI-CARANO

...nta Rosa, CA 95403   800 421.2584   707.575.7350   visit us at www.vintnersinn.com

BAKKEN CREATIVE CO.

Vintners Inn Brochure

ART DIRECTOR:	DESIGNER:	CLIENT:	TOOLS:	MATERIALS:
Michelle Bakken	Gina Mondello	Vintners Inn	Adobe Illustrator	Strathmore Pastelle

Here, having only five senses just doesn't seem fair.

Trade the weight of the world for the weight of a down duvet.

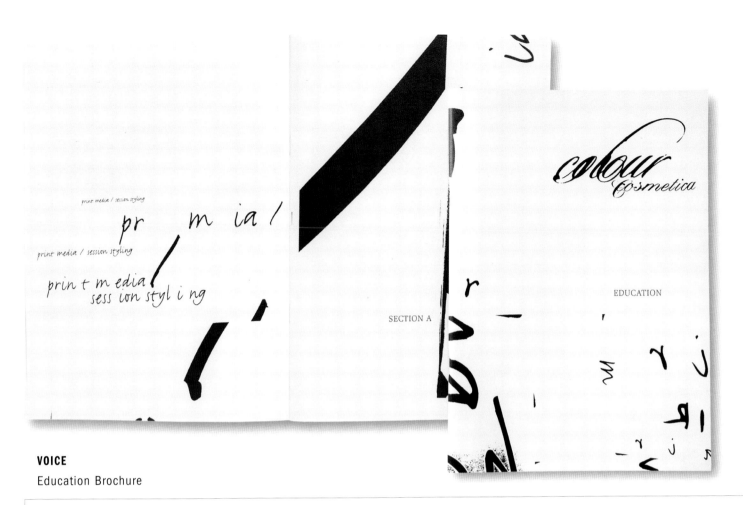

VOICE

Education Brochure

ART DIRECTORS:	DESIGNERS:	CLIENT:	TOOLS:	MATERIALS:
Anthony Deleo	Anthony Deleo	Colour Cosmetica	Macromedia Freehand	Pacesetter Laser
Scott Carslake	Scott Carslake		QuarkXPress	250 gsm (cover)
				Pacesetter Laser
				110 gsm (text)

063

ROYCROFT DESIGN

Paper Promotion

ART DIRECTOR:	DESIGNER:	CLIENT:	TOOLS:	MATERIALS:
Jennifer Roycroft	Jennifer Roycroft	Mohawk Paper Mills	QuarkXPress	50/10

JASON & JASON

Y-Point Brochure

ART DIRECTOR:	DESIGNER:	CLIENT:	TOOLS:	MATERIALS:
Jonathan Jason	Navah Uzan	RJS	Adobe Photoshop Macromedia Freehand	Chrome paper 300 gsm

Prep Academy Schools provides an environment where students can feel happy, secure and productive.

Our facilities have been designed with children in mind.

Our bright colors and whimsical decor create an uplifting and imaginative atmosphere where *creativity and learning are stimulated*.

For our younger students, an indoor athletic and play center provides a spacious, open area designed to develop large-motor and coordination skills under the guidance of a professional instructor. Physical activity is never neglected, even in inclement weather. A separate dramatic play area offers students the opportunity to engage in free-choice play.

Our state-of-the-art computer lab is available to students *at every age level*. Our skilled computer faculty teach keyboarding, educational internet use, word processing, and the latest in 'edutainment' software in daily classes beginning in preschool.

Your child's safety is our greatest concern.

Our facilities have been designed with care to provide a safe, child-oriented learning environment. We have taken every measure to provide clean, safe and secure facilities, with limited access, trained staff and administration that screen every visitor, and advanced technology to monitor all activity in the building. In addition, we are engaged in an organized, cooperative effort with local police and fire departments to educate children and their families of how to appropriately deal with potential dangers. Prep Academy Schools is constantly evaluating and upgrading our students' security.

ELEMENT—WWW.ELEMENTVILLE.COM

Prep Academy Schools Brochure

ART DIRECTOR:
Jeremy Slagle

DESIGNER:
Jeremy Slagle

CLIENT:
Prep Academy Schools

TOOLS:
Adobe InDesign
Macromedia Freehand

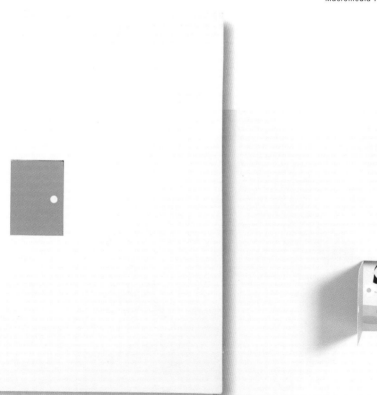

DELIVERING THE GOODS.

In the consumer mark
vation, and process in
products, and ideas fo
combines creativity ar
develop stronger bran

HORNALL ANDERSON DESIGN WORKS, INC.

Orivo Brochure

ART DIRECTOR:	DESIGNERS:	CLIENT:	TOOLS:
Jack Anderson	Andrew Wicklund	Orivo	Adobe Photoshop
	Henry Yiu		QuarkXPress

SOME ARE TIMELESS, SOME ARE FLEETING. They organize. clean. detect. monitor. bind. minimize. devour. close. save. render. destroy. regulate. pull. push. panel. instruct. carry. enclose. draw. calculate. enjoy. accelerate. defend. meld. collect. notify. support. caution. release. curtail. inform. ORIVO IS ALWAYS ASKING, WHAT IS...

NEXT?

DREAMS → REALITY

067

The historic chapel, overlooking the resort's tropical grounds and beaches, exudes an aura of romance and enchantment that is perfect for weddings and renewal of vows.

Outdoor reception areas and contemporary conference facilities provide a choice of venues for all occasions, with the assurance that One&Only Palmilla's experienced staff will create an atmosphere of impeccable service and hospitality.

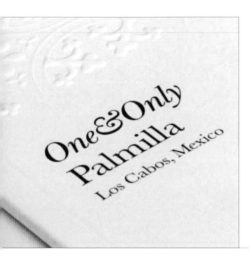

PENTAGRAM DESIGN/SF

Sales Brochure

ART DIRECTOR:	DESIGNER:	CLIENT:	TOOLS:
Brian Jacobs	Takayo Muroga	One + Only Resorts	Adobe Photoshop
			Adobe Illustrator
			QuarkXPress

A luxurious new awakening

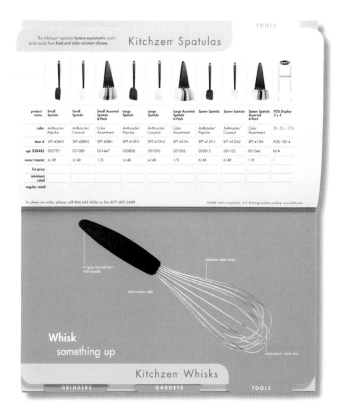

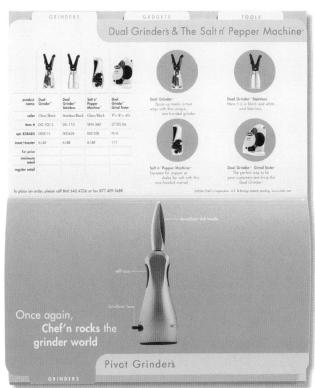

HORNALL ANDERSON DESIGN WORKS, INC.

Chef'n Catalog

ART DIRECTORS:	DESIGNERS:	CLIENT:	TOOLS:	MATERIALS:
Kathy Saito	Sonja Max	Chef'n	Adobe Photoshop	Mohawk Superfine
Jack Anderson	Alan Copeland		QuarkXPress	80 lb (cover)
Lisa Cerveny				

CF NAPA

Golden State Vineyards Brochure

ART DIRECTOR:
David Schuemann

DESIGNER:
CF Napa

CLIENT:
Golden State Vintners

TOOLS:
QuarkXPress

MATERIALS:
Paper with natural cork veneer

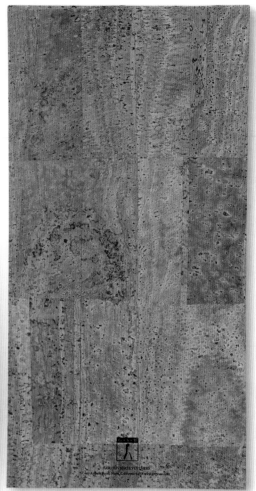

VERTICALLY INTEGRATED
fig 3
GOLDEN STATE VINTNERS

Vertical integration allows us to control quality and provide custom-tailored solutions at every step in the wine process, from growing grapes to shipping finished wines. For our outsourcing partners this means the flexibility to use Golden State Vintners' services as much as needed, at any point in the chain of production.

Outsourcing is the growing trend in the wine industry, offering winemakers and retailers better use of capital while providing the benefits of consolidation and mass efficiencies. With Golden State Vintners' vertically integrated vineyard, winery and bottling assets, our customers are assured premium quality products to which they can confidently apply their own brand marketing expertise and investment.

Hundreds of wineries in the United States and throughout the world regularly depend on Golden State Vintners for grape sourcing, wine processing services, premium varietal bulk wines, grape juice and brandy, barrel aging and storage, bottling and warehousing services. In addition, we are the premier provider of private-label wines for many of the leading retailers, restaurateurs and wholesalers across North America and in over 30 countries around the world.

Personal contact with individual customers is the hallmark of each of our service areas, as is the guarantee of exceptional quality.

ART DIRECTOR:	DESIGNER:	CLIENT:	TOOLS:	MATERIALS:
Maja Bagic	Maja Bajic	Boskinac	Adobe Photoshop	Conqueror
			Macromedia Freehand	

SALVA O'RENICK

Salva O'Renick Image Brochure

ART DIRECTOR:	DESIGNER:	CLIENT:	TOOLS:	MATERIALS:
Scott Strickler	Scott Strickler	Salva O'Renick	Adobe Photoshop QuarkXPress	NeKoosa Feltweave Carara White 100 lb (cover) Mohawk Navajo 60 lb (text)

without
noitaiveD
progress
is not
possible

Frank Zappa

Creativity. It's finding something surprising hidden within the mundane. Stepping away from protocol and playing with convention. Stretching it. Flipping it upside down. Turning it inside out until you have a perspective that's a little off kilter. But from this vantage point you discover new paths. New possibilities that lead to new thinking. New ideas that power progress. It all starts with creativity. And the courage to ask, "What if?"

Uncommonsense smashes the shackles of convention. It is a kick in the pants to uninspired thinking. It's the courage to make a difference.

072

SunBurst

Visually striking soaps created using Bradford's dual-base proprietary striation technology. Virtually any combination of additives can be incorporated into the two bases to vividly communicate a skin care benefit story.

Upbeat tone-on-tone colors were used to form Op-Art SunBurst patterns. In the SingleStripe examples, a dazzling background was created using light reflective and light bending particles in our vegetable translucent base. Cheerful primary colored opaque stripes race down the middle of each bar.

WEYMOUTH DESIGN

Bradford TrendScape Brochure

ART DIRECTOR:	DESIGNERS:	CLIENT:	TOOLS:	MATERIALS:
Tom Laidlaw	Arvi Raquel-Santos	Bradford Soap	QuarkXPress	Sappi McCoy Silk
	Brad Lewthwaite	Works, Inc.		

Eco-Ex

Totally natural, uncolored, unfragranced soaps produced through the saponification of unusual blends of oils known to have beneficial effects on the skin, Eco-Ex is one of Bradford's new generation of soap bases. These formulas lather beautifully and leave the skin feeling silky soft.

Tuscan Blend - Saponified from hazelnut, walnut, almond and coconut oils.

Polynesian Blend - Saponified from kukui nut, macadamia, almond and coconut oils.

Blue Ridge Mountain Blend - Saponified from pecan, walnut, peanut and coconut oils.

Moroccan Blend - Saponified from cashew, pistachio, walnut and coconut oils.

073

PRODUCTS | SERVICES

Baby Talk

The Target® Guest will not only pass-on her hazel eyes and curly hair to her new baby, she'll also pass along her sense of style, she'll choose her baby's outfits as carefully as she chooses her own. She'll start encouraging her baby's interests at an early age and make sure her surroundings are safe as well as nurturing. Baby will go wherever mommy does: Shopping, out to lunch and sometimes to work. Don't be surprised to find them both in baby aerobics class.

The Target Lullaby Club® has welcomed more than 4,000,000 bundles of joy.

40% of guests have children under 18 at home.

40% of guests with children have children under 6.

22% are between 18 and 34 years old.

GRAPHICULTURE

Getting to Know . . .

ART DIRECTOR:	CLIENT:	TOOLS:	MATERIALS:
Cheryl Watson	Target	Adobe Illustrator QuarkXPress	dull coated stock

Who is The Core Guest?

Who shops at Target®? The answer is both simple and complex. She's a unique individual (80% are female) who's upscale (median household income of $54,000) and educated (40% have graduated from a 4-year college). When she's not working, you'll find her in her suburban home raising a family (40% have children) and pursuing a variety of interests (41% enjoy gardening). But she's much more than statistics. She's style conscious and aware of trends. She values her time and her opinions. And her life is about to change in a big way. Get to know her and you'll know what she's looking for.

Getting to know the Target® Guest

Creating Experiences with Audio Architecture™

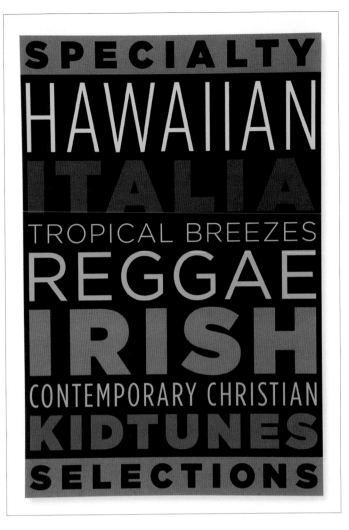

PENTAGRAM DESIGN/SF

Capabilities Brochure

ART DIRECTOR:	DESIGNER:	CLIENT:	TOOLS:
Kit Hinrichs	Laura Scott	Muzak	Adobe Photoshop
			Adobe Illustrator
			QuarkXPress

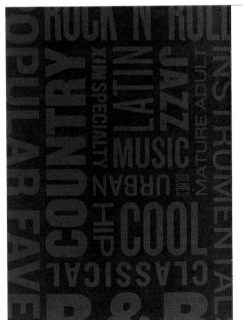

Music. Some people call it our passion. Others, our obsession. Inspired by the art of Audio Architecture, Muzak gives you more than just music. We give you music that creates an experience—a powerful experience, a persuasive experience, an experience that captures the image, energy and soul of your business. Our music builds a connection with listeners that is centered in their hearts and held in their memories. It's an emotional force, making what your customers hear as important as what they see or touch. Our motivation is to put that force to work in a meaningful way. We do it for thousands of clients every day. We'd like to do the same for you. Enough said. Let's take a listen.

Audio Architecture integrates Music, Voice and Sound Systems to create experiences that build emotional connections with your customers.

075

We'd like to talk to you about insurance. But we know you'd probably rather talk about your family, your job, your vacation, your home team, your neighbors, your recipe for lasagna, your boat, your dreams, your hobbies, your aunt, your dog, your cat, your llama, your shoes, your favorite restaurant or almost anything else. **So we'll be brief.**

HORNALL ANDERSON DESIGN WORKS, INC.

Safeco Corporate Brochure

ART DIRECTORS:	DESIGNERS:	DESIGNERS:	CLIENT:
Jack Anderson	Larry Anderson	Holly Craven	Safeco Corporation
Larry Anderson	Jay Hilburn	John Anderle	
		Erin McFarlan	

Okay, we're excited.

Auto: Cars are complicated. Automatically reducing the premium on your insurance as soon as you qualify is one way we're trying to make it easier.

24/7 Claim Service. [...]

Easy Repair Options. [...]

Home: What is your home worth today? We eliminate the worry by making it easy for you to insure your home for 100% of its replacement value.

Tailored Coverage. [...]

Extended Dwelling Coverage. [...]

Really?

Yes. We know you are much more excited about the things you own than the insurance you protect them with. So we want the process of buying and owning insurance to be as easy for you as possible. One word sums it up: uncomplicate. And it starts now.

THE POINT GROUP

Upscale Development Introductory Brochure

ART DIRECTOR:	**DESIGNER:**	**CLIENT:**	**TOOLS:**	**MATERIALS:**
David Howard	Cassandra Zimmerman	Victory Dallas	Adobe Photoshop	Mohawk Options
			QuarkXPress	

feel the rush

Connecting the city's many high-energy districts, Victory is a major traffic generator with three million visitors per year and over 500,000 vehicles passing by daily.

UPTOWN
the urban, trendy and intellectual scene in Dallas.

DOWNTOWN
the epicenter of the Metroplex, with a revitalizing nightlife district.

WEST END
entertainment venues and historic attractions luring unsuspecting tourists to the center of the city.

ARTS DISTRICT
the cultural and magnetic mix of art and music combine here in the nation's largest urban arts district.

FASHION/DESIGN DISTRICT
fashion events amidst a treasure trove of unique interior design pieces.

giddy up

It's not about big hair or cowboy hats. The cultured, affluent and fashion-forward of Dallas thrive on excitement and atmosphere. This is the place that shakes things up – this isn't J.R.'s Dallas.

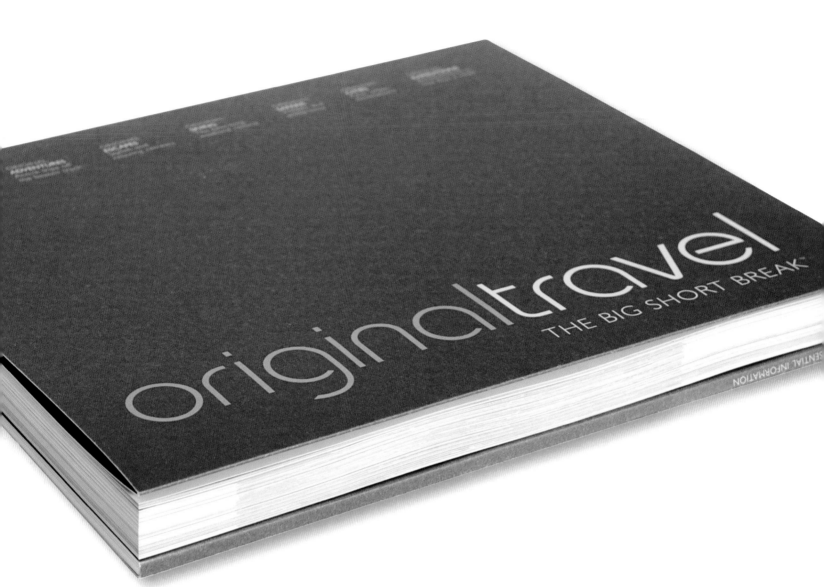

originalsafaris

FROM THE KENYAN SAVANNAH TO THE OKAVANGO DELTA IN BOTSWANA, AFRICA HAS A HUGE VARIETY OF INSPIRING SAFARI DESTINATIONS.

Overnight flights and minimal time difference mean deep sea fishing off the coast of Mozambique is now a long weekend possibility. Sample a selection of the continent's most original and hidden destinations: see dawn rise over the Namib Desert from a hot air balloon; watch chimpanzees playing in the rainforests of Tanzania or dive the beautiful coral gardens of the Red Sea.

DESTINATION	THE TRIP	PAGE
BOTSWANA	Okavango Delta safari	114
EGYPT	Red Sea safari	116
KENYA	Bush & beach	120
MOZAMBIQUE	Indian Ocean diving & fishing	124
NAMIBIA	Desert safari	126
SOUTH AFRICA	Sabi Sands safari	128
TANZANIA	Chimp safari	130
	Bush & beach	132
UGANDA	Gorilla safari	134

INARIA

Travel Brochure

ART DIRECTOR:
Debora Berardi

DESIGNERS:
Debora Berardi
Andrew Thomas

CLIENT:
Original Travel

TOOLS:
Adobe Photoshop
Adobe Illustrator
QuarkXPress

MATERIALS:
Hello Silk
Challenger Offset

CONTENTS

ORIGINAL ADVENTURES
20 CROATIA
22 FRANCE
26 ICELAND
30 JORDAN
34 MOROCCO
38 NORWAY
44 OMAN
48 PORTUGAL
50 SWEDEN
54 TURKEY
60 ZAMBIA

ORIGINAL ESCAPES
66 FRANCE
74 GOZO
76 ITALY
84 MADEIRA
86 MONTENEGRO
90 SOUTH AFRICA
92 SPAIN
96 SWEDEN
100 UK

ORIGINAL SKIING
106 AUSTRIA
108 ITALY
109 SWEDEN
109 SWITZERLAND
110 FRANCE

ORIGINAL SAFARIS
114 BOTSWANA
116 EGYPT
120 KENYA
122 MOZAMBIQUE
126 NAMIBIA
130 SOUTH AFRICA
132 TANZANIA
138 UGANDA

ORIGINAL CITIES
144 BEIRUT
145 BERLIN
148 CAPETOWN
149 COPENHAGEN
150 DUBROVNIK
151 ISTANBUL
152 LISBON
153 MARRAKECH
156 NEWYORK
157 RIO DE JANEIRO
158 ROME
159 SEVILLE
162 STOCKHOLM
163 TALLINN
164 VENICE

ORIGINAL EXPEDITIONS
168 FRANCE
176 NORWAY
178 TANZANIA

079

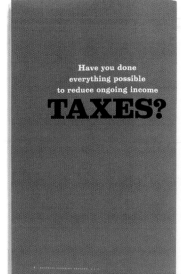

TANAGRAM PARTNERS

Business Planning Systems
Capabilities Brochure

ART DIRECTOR:
Grant Davis

CLIENT:
Business Planning
Systems

MATERIALS:
Mohawk Superfine
Eggshell

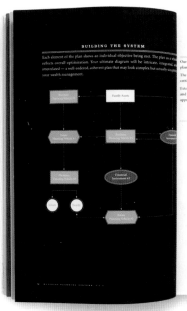

THE POINT GROUP

Upscale Real Estate Brochure

ART DIRECTOR:
David Howard

DESIGNER:
Cassandra Zimmerman

CLIENT:
W Hotel & Residences

TOOLS:
Adobe Photoshop
Adobe Illustrator
QuarkXPress

MATERIALS:
Domtar Solutions
Carrera white

Getting your message across the world is no easy task. There are many potential pitfalls. It's easy to use the wrong inflection, cause offence, or waste your money. When you're co-ordinating people and projects thousands of miles away, there's plenty of scope for misunderstandings.

Verbatim provides a total solution for companies who want to make their words count in different countries. Though we pride ourselves on the quality of our translation services, our comprehensive language management offer goes much further than just the words. It includes planning, production, logistics and distribution. So we can take a project all the way from the drawing board and right into your target audience's hands.

With Verbatim, you can be sure your words say the right thing at the right time.

> **Could your life be made easier?**
Few companies have the capability or resources to manage international communications. As well as careful co-ordination, they need local knowledge and dedicated teams in different parts of the world. But Verbatim knows how to smooth the whole process. We're experts in the field, and bring continuity and efficiency to even the most complex projects. Deal with us, and we can deal with everything else for you.

HAT-TRICK DESIGN
Verbatim Brochure

ART DIRECTORS:	DESIGNERS:	CLIENT:	TOOLS:	MATERIALS:
Gareth Howat	Jim Sutherland	Verbatim	Adobe Photoshop	Skye Brilliant White
David Kimpton	Adam Giles		QuarkXPress	
Jim Sutherland				

KEEP RIGHT

the business of language.   verbatim.

> **Are your words digestible?**
Mistranslations can be entertaining ('frozen codpiece' anybody?). But not when they affect your business. Verbatim makes sure that your messages come across loud, clear and consistently in different territories, in any media. This immediately shows you're serious, switched on and thorough. After all, the quality of your communication is a reflection of the quality of your product.

Please
Disturb

S'il Vous Plait Déranger

Stören Sie Bitte

Se Ruega Molestar

> **Do you mean what you say?**
Tone, nuance and emphasis can easily get lost in translation, which is why Verbatim sources its translators so carefully. We use local mother-tongue translators with relevant technical and industry knowledge. And we learn from each project, building glossaries of technical terms and specialist words and phrases that may crop up in the future.

MARIUS FAHRNER DESIGN

Kitchen Brochure for a Designer

ART DIRECTOR:	DESIGNER:	CLIENT:	TOOLS:	MATERIALS:
Marius Fahrner	Marius Fahrner	Ulrike Urages	Macromedia Freehand	Noblesse 300 g naturel Classen Paper (cover) Maxi Satin 200 g white Igepa (text)

083

USINE DE BOUTONS

TRAVEL BOOK

ART DIRECTOR:
Lionello Borean

DESIGNERS:
Lionello Borean
Chiara Grandesso

CLIENT:
INVICTA SpA

TOOLS:
Adobe Illustrator

NO.PARKING

Presentation Brochure for Franchising Store (single sheets and folder)

ART DIRECTOR:	DESIGNER:	CLIENT:	TOOLS:	MATERIALS:
Caterina Romino	Caterina Romino	Iojo—Body Objects	QuarkXPress	Magnomatt 120 g

ANTFARM INC. (CHANGING TO KAMPER BRANDS)

Stevens Square Condos

DESIGNERS:	CLIENT:	TOOLS:
Dan Behrens	Real Estate Development	Adobe Photoshop
Patrick Crowe	Group	Adobe Illustrator

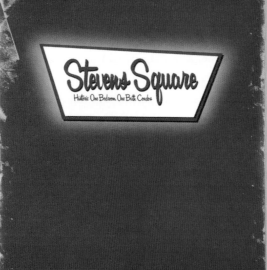

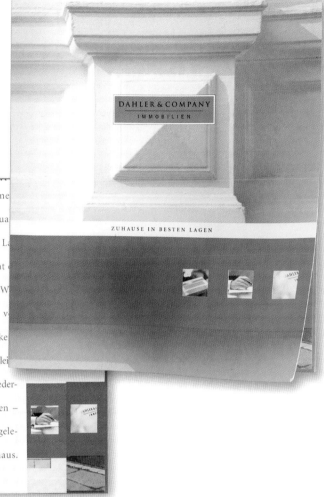

Dürfen wir Sie herzlich willkomme[n] heißen? Schließlich sind wir jetzt qua[si] Nachbarn. Denn wer in den besten L[a]gen der schönsten Städte wohnt, hat e[s] zu Dahler & Company nicht weit. W[ir] sind die Spe- zialisten v[or] Ort. Die, die sich auske[n]nen, die ihr Domizil glei[ch] in Ihrer Nähe haben und die Ihnen jederzeit mit Rat und Tat beiseite stehen – soweit es Immobilien betrifft und gelegentlich auch einmal darüber hinaus. Schnell, diskret und kompetent.

MARIUS FAHRNER DESIGN

Real Estate Company Image Brochure

ART DIRECTOR:	DESIGNER:	TOOLS:	MATERIALS:
Marius Fahrner	Marius Fahrner	Macromedia Freehand	Igepa Soporset 170–300 g

087

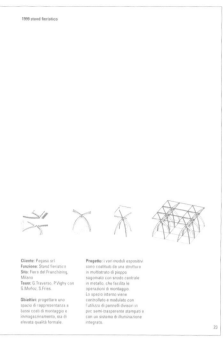

1999 stand fieristico

Cliente: Pegaso srl
Funzione: Stand fieristico
Sito: Fiera del Franchising, Milano
Team: G.Traverso, P.Vighy con G.Muñoz, S.Fries.

Obiettivi: progettare uno spazio di rappresentanza a bassi costi di montaggio e immagazzinamento, ma di elevata qualità formale.

Progetto: i vari moduli espositivi sono costituiti da una struttura in multistrato di pioppo sagomato con snodo centrale in metallo, che facilita le operazioni di montaggio. Lo spazio interno viene controllato e modulato con l'utilizzo di pannelli divisori in pvc semi-trasparente stampati e con un sistema di illuminazione integrato.

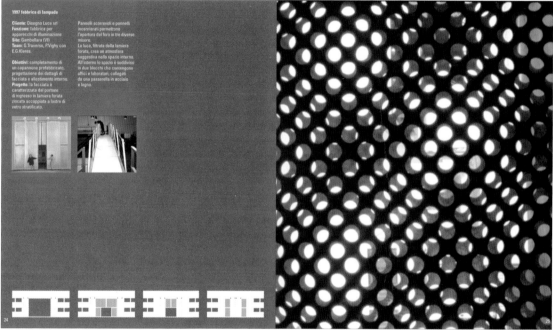

1997 fabbrica di lampade

Cliente: Disegno Luce srl
Funzione: fabbrica per apparecchi di illuminazione
Sito: Gambellara (VI)
Team: G.Traverso, P.Vighy con E.G.Kleres.

Obiettivi: completamento di un capannone prefabbricato, progettazione dei dettagli di facciata e allestimento interno.
Progetto: la facciata è caratterizzata dal portone di ingresso in lamiera forata zincata accoppiata a lastre di vetro stratificato.

Pannelli scorrevoli e pannelli incernierati permettono l'apertura del foro in tre diverse misure.
Le luce, filtrata dalla lamiera forata, crea un'atmosfera suggestiva nello spazio interno.
All'interno lo spazio è suddiviso in due blocchi che contengono uffici e laboratori, collegati da una passerella in acciaio e legno.

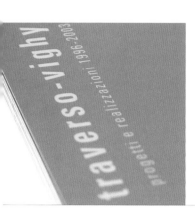

NO.PARKING

Exhibition Catalogue Illustrating the Works
of the Architects "Traverso & Vighy"

ART DIRECTOR:	DESIGNER:	CLIENT:	TOOLS:	MATERIALS:
Caterina Romino	Elisa Dall'Angelo	Traverso & Vighy	QuarkXPress	Magnomatt 100 g 48 pages

**ANTFARM INC.
(CHANGING TO KAMPER BRANDS)**

Rossmor True Lofts

DESIGNERS:	CLIENT:	TOOLS:	MATERIALS:
Dan Behrens	PAK Properties	Adobe Photoshop	four-color process
Patrick Crowe		Adobe Illustrator	Pantone 877
			spot varnish

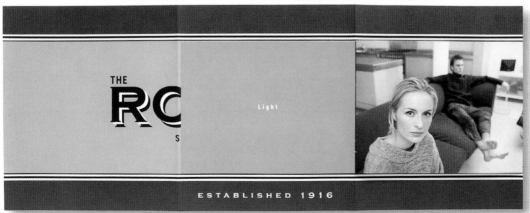

butter
cheese
~~cream~~
~~milk~~
new new dairy culture
yogurt

Dairy
The food of life

PERKS DESIGN PARTNERS

Dairy Culture Educational Kit

ART DIRECTOR:	**DESIGNER:**	**CLIENT:**	**TOOLS:**
Chris Perks	Maurice Lai	Dairy Australia	Adobe Illustrator
			QuarkXPress

090

IMAGINE

2 Busy Pack

ART DIRECTOR:	DESIGNER:	CLIENT:	TOOLS:
David Caunce	David Caunce	2 Busy-Lifestyle Management	Adobe Illustrator QuarkXPress

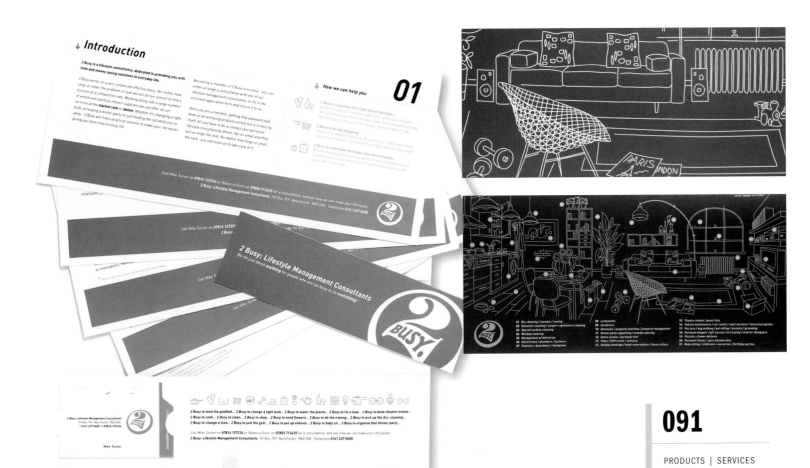

SKIN BIOLOGY CENTER - PFLEGE FÜR DIE HAUT

Gerade in den letzten Jahren hat die dermatologische Forschung neue, umfassende Erkenntnisse über die Haut des Menschen in ihrer faszinierenden Vielfalt und großen Individualität gewonnen. Dies erweitert die Möglichkeiten zur Behandlung, Gesunderhaltung und Vitalisierung unseres grössten Organs. Gezielte Hautpflege, konsequenter Hautschutz, Prävention von Hautschäden sowie die Verbesserung des Hautzustandes aus ästhetisch-dermatologischer Sicht bilden die Kernkompetenz des SBC.
Das Institut wurde 1999 auf Initiative des Hamburger Dermatologen Prof. Dr. Volker Steinkraus im denkmalgeschützten Bau der ehemaligen Alten Oberpostdirektion am Stephansplatz gegründet. In hellen, puristisch gestalteten Räumen arbeiten erfahrene Kosmetikerinnen gemeinsam mit beratenden Dermatologen an der Verwirklichung eines Rundum-Verwöhn- und Pflegeprogramms für Haut, Körper und Geist.

Zum Spektrum der Behandlungen gehören neben kosmetischen Intensivbehandlungen für Gesicht und Körper moderne Methoden zur Verjüngung und Glättung der Haut.

Pures Wohlbefinden und eine gepflegte und tiefengereinigte Haut sind das Resultat jeder Behandlung im Skin Biology Center.

MARIUS FAHRNER DESIGN
Cosmetic Institute

ART DIRECTOR:	DESIGNER:	CLIENT:	TOOLS:	MATERIALS:
Marius Fahrner	Marius Fahrner	Skin Biology Center - Hamburg	Macromedia Freehand	Maxi Satin Igepa 250 g 170 g

PERMANENT BEAUTY – CONTURE MAKE-UP

Durch die schonungsvolle Methode des Conture Make up, auch Permanent Make up genannt, ist es möglich, feinste Farbpigmente in die Haut zu implantieren. Ob Augenbrauen, Lidstriche oder Lippenkonturen, das Arbeiten mit einer hauchfeinen Akupunkturnadel garantiert millimetergenaues Pigmentieren für ein natürliches und schönes Basis Make-up. Auch verletzungs- oder krankheitsbedingte Haut- und Haarprobleme können durch diese Methode permanent abgedeckt werden.

IDAS – INTERDISZIPLINÄRE ANTI-AGING SPRECHSTUNDE

Nach einer von Professor Steinkraus eigens entwickelten Systematik werden in der IDAS moderne Techniken des sogenannten Anti-Aging zur Vitalisierung des gesamten Organismus aufgezeigt, kritisch betrachtet und bedarfsgerecht angewendet. Dabei steht nicht nur die Haut im Vordergrund, sondern das Erkennen von vermeidbaren Risikofaktoren für eine vorzeitige Alterung des Organismus und Erkrankungen aller Art. Die wichtigsten Prämissen der IDAS sind "Safety First", das unbedingte Festhalten an der eigenen Authentizität sowie eine kritische Haltung gegenüber nicht Evidenz-basierten Methoden.

S·B·C | SKIN BIOLOGY CENTER

GRAPHICULTURE

Swell—Simple Solutions

ART DIRECTOR:	CLIENT:	TOOLS:	MATERIALS:
Cheryl Watson	Target	Adobe Photoshop	coated paper
		Adobe Illustrator	
		QuarkXPress	

S amantha, can I see you in the kitchen, please? Always be poised to whip out a happy meal — make it an informal picnic of leftovers and takeout surprise, pulled together at the last minute. The three magic words: keep it simple.

"Kids! Dinner!"
swell melamine dinnerware, .99–$9.99 table linens, .99–$19.99

1 n the swell dictionary, "cozy" and "comfy" are not synonyms for "just fell asleep in the laundry hamper." Have a little swell something in the closet for the nights you want to be snuggly and a hottie.

"Better than counting sheep!"
chemise, $14.99

TRACY DESIGN COMMUNICATIONS
Jennifer-Anne Promotional Brochure

ART DIRECTOR:	DESIGNER:	CLIENT:	TOOLS:
Jan Tracy	Patrick Simon	Jennifer-Anne	Adobe Illustrator
			QuarkXPress

094

INARIA

Restaurant Brochure

ART DIRECTOR:	DESIGNERS:	CLIENT:	TOOLS:	MATERIALS:
Andrew Thomas	Andrew Thomas	Mosaico	Adobe Photoshop	Colourplan
	Debora Berardi		Adobe Illustrator	Hello Silk
			QuarkXPress	

Heavenly dishes

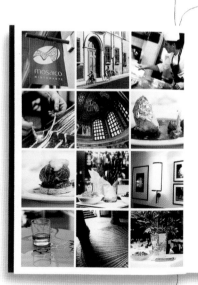

Inspired by tradition

ART DIRECTOR:	DESIGNER:	CLIENT:	TOOLS:
Kit Hinrichs	Laura Scott	Muzak	Adobe Photoshop
			Adobe Illustrator
			QuarkXPress

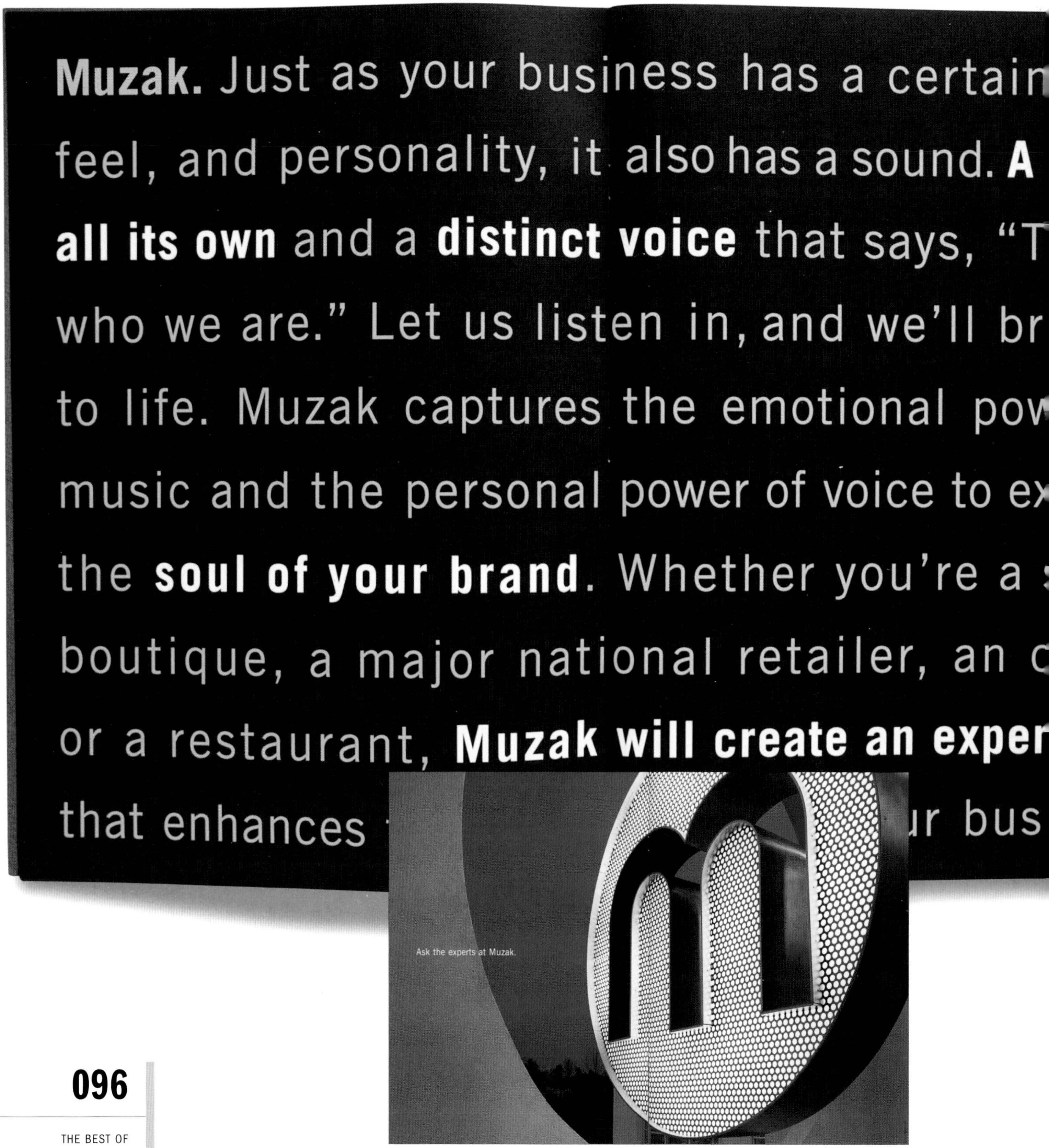

Muzak. Just as your business has a certain feel, and personality, it also has a sound. **A** **all its own** and a **distinct voice** that says, "T who we are." Let us listen in, and we'll br to life. Muzak captures the emotional pov music and the personal power of voice to e the **soul of your brand**. Whether you're a boutique, a major national retailer, an c or a restaurant, **Muzak will create an exper** that enhances ur bus

Ask the experts at Muzak.

What does a leather loafer sound like?

What does your business sound like?

What does aged parmigiano sound like?

Search

DISCERNING GUESTS DESERVE
DISTINGUISHED TEAS

BAILEY/FRANKLIN

Teas of Origin Brochure

ART DIRECTORS:	**DESIGNERS:**	**CLIENT:**	**TOOLS:**	**MATERIALS:**
Dan Franklin	Connie Lightner	Boyd Coffe Company	Adobe Photoshop	Vintage Velvet
Connie Lightner	Dan Franklin		QuarkXPress	

TO CLAIM THE DIFFERENCE
CLAIM TEAS OF ORIGIN

ART DIRECTOR:	DESIGNER:	CLIENT:	TOOLS:	MATERIALS:
Lawrence Hennessy	Lawrence Hennessy	Australian Consolidated Press (ACP)	Adobe Illustrator QuarkXPress	Nimbus Perigord

POMME STUDIO

Eight Promotional Brochures for Sales Reps

ART DIRECTOR:	DESIGNER:	CLIENT:	TOOLS:	MATERIALS:
Pamela Zuccker	Pamela Zuccker	Larson-Juhl	QuarkXPress	Storaenso Productolith matte

STYLE NOTEBOOK

Palette Invite the outside world indoors with an earthy palette of grounding colors.

Rock and Stone A mixture of stacked stone, river rock or slate provides a sense of history and permanence.

Native Timber Balcony railings crafted from gnarled and knotted tree limbs; handcrafted rustic furniture adorned with coverings of white birch bark and decorated with intricate patterns of twig appliqué; and exposed beams of rough-hewn wood are all staples in this natural setting.

Forged Iron The long-standing appeal of iron comes from its natural and honest character. Unpretentious and rugged, it's an important element in decorative accessories.

Art and Framing Create thematic displays that tie into the outdoors by displaying framed leaves, dried flowers or fishing flies. Also consider weathered maps and trail guides that remind you of special places you have traveled.

Taking its cue from nature, the frame's warm, pine finish and detailed roping are in perfect harmony with the art and the lodge decor.

Fishing flies from Blue Quill Angler framed in the Pine River Collection.

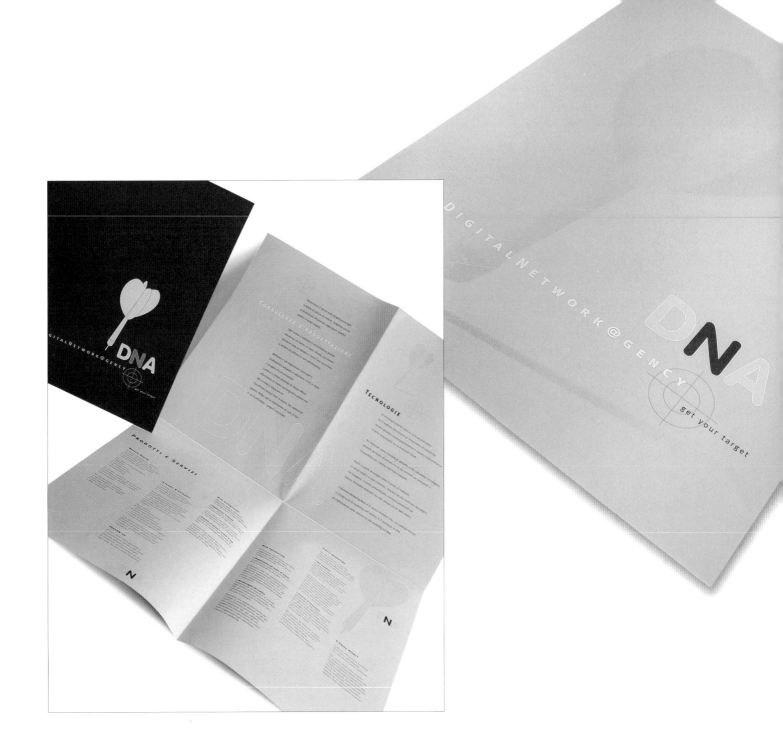

NO.PARKING

Folded Brochure/Poster

ART DIRECTOR:	DESIGNER:	CLIENT:	TOOLS:	MATERIALS:
Sabine Lercher	Sabine Lercher	DNA—Digital Internet Agency	QuarkXPress	Magnomatt 100 g

PENTAGRAM DESIGN/SF

Sales Brochure

ART DIRECTOR:
Brian Jacobs

DESIGNER:
Takayo Muroga

CLIENT:
One + Only Resorts

TOOLS:
Adobe Photoshop
Adobe Illustrator
QuarkXPress

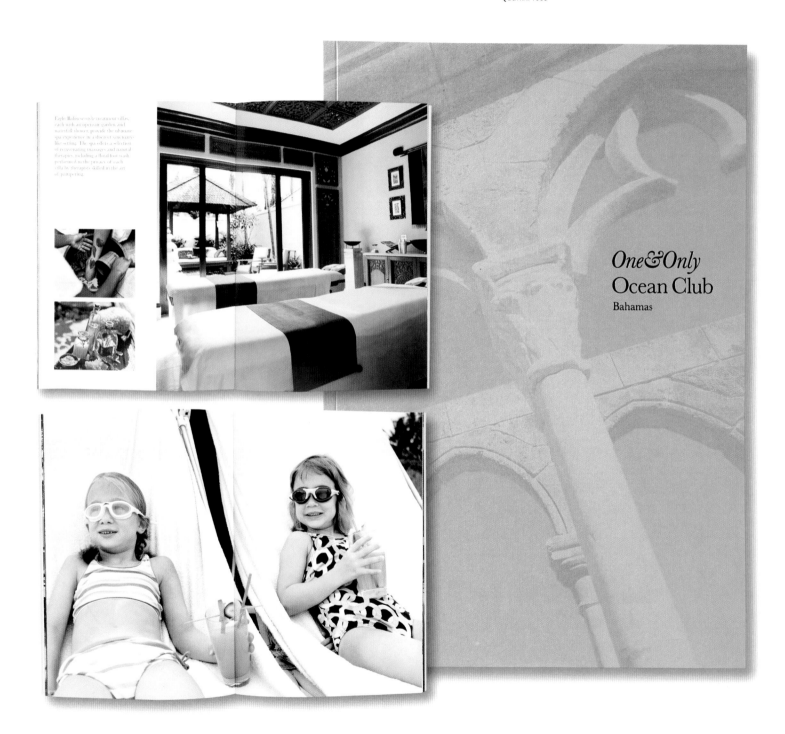

CACAO DESIGN

Events Menu/Brochure

ART DIRECTOR:	DESIGNER:	CLIENT:	TOOLS:
Creative Team	Anna Carbone	Tribu	Adobe InDesign

103

NO.PARKING

Product Catalog

ART DIRECTOR:	DESIGNER:	CLIENT:	TOOLS:	MATERIALS:
Elisa Dall'Angelo	Elisa Dall'Angelo	ETA—chair production company	QuarkXPress	Magnomatt 100 g (cover) cardboard spiral bound

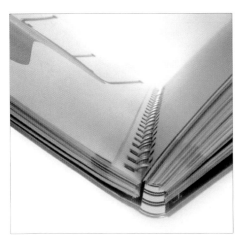

HIPPO STUDIO

WOW Product Brochure

ART DIRECTORS:	DESIGNERS:	PHOTOGRAPHER:	CLIENT:	TOOLS:
William Ho Siu Chuen	William Ho Siu Chuen	Addy KC Cheung	JIA	Adobe Photoshop
Chin Lee Ma	Chin Lee Ma			Adobe Illustrator
	Jeffery Wong			

The "Second Skin" is a unique
element in our design.
After the foam has been attached to
the frame a cotton cover is added.
This protects and holds the various
foams used in shape,
and allows the easy dressing and
removal of the fabric cover.

SAVAS CEKIC DESIGN OFFICE
Prestige Brochure

ART DIRECTOR: DESIGNER: CLIENT: TOOLS: MATERIALS:
Savas Cekic   Savas Cekic   Danca Design Furniture   Macromedia Freehand   Zanders

The scientific data recorded
in design literature as the
linguistic,
semiotic and semantic,
reveals itself in a flower stem.

A single rose
or a country bouquet,
or tulips replace
a thousand meanings.

Danca
speaks nature's
language.

Tasman Bay Olives Ltd incorporates three olive groves : Beulah Olives, Nelson Olive Grove and Bethany Olive Grove, all situated on the Moutere clays in the Tasman Bay region of New Zealand. The Moutere clay is gaining increasing recognition for producing superior flavour for many types of horticultural crops such as wine, apples, and olives. The combination of these ideal growing conditions and high sunshine in the Nelson area results in a premium quality olive oil.

Tasman Bay Olives is primarily focused on the premium Italian varieties. Tests by the Cawthron Institute on Elovi Olive Oil show low acidity levels of between 0.05% to 0.17%.

New Zealand Freshness with an Italian Flavour

ELOVI | OLIVE | OIL

the best of both worlds

LLOYDS GRAPHIC DESIGN LTD

Olive Oil Producer Promotional Brochure

ART DIRECTOR:	DESIGNER:	CLIENT:	TOOLS:	MATERIALS:
Alexander Lloyd	Alexander Lloyd	Tasman Bay Olives/Elovi Olive Oil	Adobe Photoshop Macromedia Freehand	matte textured stock 220 gsm

107

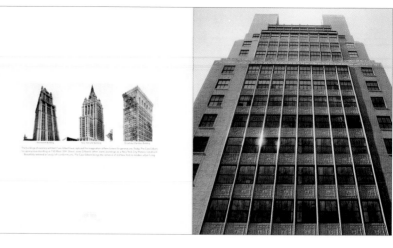

LISKA + ASSOCIATES, INC.

The Cass Gilbert Brochure

ART DIRECTOR:	DESIGNERS:	CLIENT:	TOOLS:	MATERIALS:
Tanya Quick	Tanya Quick	Douglas Elliman	Adobe Photoshop	Mohawk Superfine soft
	Fernando Munoz	The Cass Gilbert	Adobe Illustrator	white smooth 100 lb
			QuarkXPress	(cover)

THE BEST OF
BROCHURE DESIGN 8

MODELHART GRAFIK-DESIGN

Brochure for Meissl Large Umbrellas

ART DIRECTOR:	DESIGNER:	CLIENT:	TOOLS:	MATERIALS:
Herbert O. Modelhart	Herbert O. Modelhart	Meissl GmbH	Adobe Photoshop	Tom & Otto art paper
			Adobe Illustrator	double silk coated
			QuarkXPress	

109

USINE DE BOUTONS

TEKWAY

ART DIRECTOR:	DESIGNERS:	CLIENT:	TOOLS:
Lionello Borean	Lionello Borean Chiara Grandesso	INVICTA SpA	Adobe Illustrator

NONPROFIT | EDUCATIONAL
INSTITUTIONAL

DPARTNERS TOMATOKOŠIRCDP GEORGETSCHERNYINCNESNADNY+SHWAR
ICKDESIGNREDPATH VOICERUTGERSUNIVERSITYNASSARDESIGNINARIAPERKSDES
TNERSCONCRETEDANIELLEFOUSHÉEDESIGN MIRKOILICCORP
TOFFINEARTSBOSTONHAMMERPRESSANDPARTNERSALTERPOPTOMATOKOŠIRCDPWATTSDESIGNE
CHERNYINCNESNADNY+SHWARTZHATTRICKDESIGNREDPATHFLIGHTCREATIVEVOICERUTGERSUNIV
INARIAPERKSDESIGNPARTNERSCONCRETEDANIELLEFOUSHÉEDESIGNSTORMVISUAL
UNICATIONSINCMIRKOILICCORPMUSEUMOFFINEARTSBOSTONANDPARTNER
ATOKOŠIRCDP GEORGETSCHERNYINCNESNADNY+SHWARTZHATTRICKDESIGNREDPA
VOICERUTGERSUNIVERSITYNASSARDESIGNINARIA PERKSDESIGNPARTNERSCONCRE
ELLEFOUSHÉEDESIGN MIRKOILICCORPMUSEUMOFFINEARTSB
AMMERPRESSANDPARTNERSALTERPOPTOMATOKOŠIRCDPWATTSDESIGNGEORGETSCHERNYINCNE
+SHWARTZHATTRICKDESIGNREDPATHFLIGHTCREATIVEVOICERUTGERSUNIVERSITY
ERKSDESIGNPARTNERSCONCRETEDANIELLEFOUSHÉEDESIGNSTORMVISUAL COMMUNICATIONSINC
ICCORPMUSEUMOFFINEARTSBOSTONANDPARTNERS TOMATOKOŠIRCDP
ESIGNGEORGETSCHERNYINCNESNADNY+SHWARTZ REDPATHFLIGHTCREATIVE VOI
ERSUNIVERSITYNASSARDESIGN PERKSDESIGNPARTNERSCONCRETE DANIELLEFOUSHÉEDES
MIRKOILICCORPMUSEUMOFFINEARTSBOSTON
ALTERPOPTOMATOKOŠIRCDPWATTSDESIGNGEORGETSCHERNYINCNESNADNY+SHWARTZHAT

Laws restricting abortion pose serious risks to women. In the two decades before abortion was legalized in the US, as many as 1.2 million women per year sought illegal "back alley" abortions. Thousands died. Tens of thousands suffered serious medical injury.

Medically safe, legal abortion has had a profound effect on the health and well being of American women. Today, abortion is nearly twice as safe as a penicillin injection.

IT'S ABOUT TIME

BenchMark
NCJW's Campaign to Save Roe

NCJW'S VOICE:
THE VOICE OF THE JEWISH COMMUNITY

FOR OVER A CENTURY THE NATIONAL COUNCIL OF JEWISH WOMEN HAS BEEN AT THE FOREFRONT OF SOCIAL CHANGE—COURAGEOUSLY TAKING A PROGRESSIVE STANCE ON ISSUES SUCH AS REPRODUCTIVE FREEDOM. TODAY, NCJW IS THE LEADING JEWISH ORGANIZATION FIGHTING TO PROTECT THAT FREEDOM.

As Jews, we understand what it means to have fundamental rights and liberties stripped away.

WE CANNOT BE SILENT ON THIS ISSUE

92% OF THE JEWISH COMMUNITY **IS PRO-CHOICE**

IT IS TIME TO BRING THE POWER AND THE VOICE OF THAT COMMUNITY TOGETHER

Reproductive rights are closely tied to religious freedom. Women have the right to be respected as moral decision-makers, able to make choices based on their own beliefs and traditions. For the courts to impose one religion's view on all of us defies the very meaning of religious liberty.

NCJW'S BENCHMARK
ALREADY TAKING ACTI

EDUCATING AND MOBILIZING THOUS,

LEADING PRO-CHOICE RALLIES AND ACROSS THE COUNTRY

BUILDING STATE COALITIONS

FLYING KEY LEADERS AND SPEAKERS TO MEET WITH SENATORS

EMPOWERING ONLINE ACTIVISTS VIA AN INTERACTIVE WEB SITE

NOW, IT'S YO
LOG ON TO WWW.BENCHM
AND JOIN BENCHMARK TOD

ART DIRECTOR:	DESIGNER:	CLIENT:	TOOLS:	MATERIALS:
David Schimmel	Susan Brzozowski	National Council of Jewish Women	Adobe Photoshop QuarkXPress	Productolith

THE EROSION OF FREEDOM IS A SLIPPERY SLOPE. IF WE LOSE REPRODUCTIVE RIGHTS, OTHER CORE RIGHTS—LIKE RELIGIOUS LIBERTY AND CIVIL RIGHTS—MAY BE CLOSE BEHIND.

THE FUTURE WILL BE SET BY JUDGES WHO HOLD LIFETIME SEATS ON THE FEDERAL BENCH. ANTI-CHOICE JUDGES ARE ALREADY ATTACKING THE RIGHT TO ABORTION. AND MORE ANTI-CHOICE NOMINEES ARE WAITING IN THE WINGS—POSITIONED TO RENDER DECISIONS THAT WILL DEFINE FREEDOM FOR GENERATIONS TO COME.

The President openly admires staunch anti-choice jurists and is nominating extremists to the federal bench. Senators have a constitutional duty to independently evaluate such nominees. Yet, they have been pressured to rush their decision-making and have, on occasion, been bypassed entirely.

FIND YOUR VOICE. IT'S TIME TO SPEAK OUT AND FIGHT BACK. ON JANUARY 22, 1973 THE SUPREME COURT AFFIRMED WOMEN'S CONSTITUTIONAL RIGHT TO ABORTION IN ITS LANDMARK *ROE V. WADE* RULING. TODAY THIS RIGHT IS UNDER ATTACK IN COURTROOMS ACROSS THE COUNTRY. YOU CAN DO SOMETHING ABOUT IT. TAKE ACTION TODAY, BEFORE IT'S TOO LATE.

GN IS

PLE

EVENTS

GTON, DC

DATES, AND

TURN

PAIGN.ORG

115

NONPROFIT | EDUCATIONAL
INSTITUTIONAL

ART DIRECTOR:	DESIGNER:	CLIENT:	TOOLS:	MATERIALS:
Tomato Kosir	Tomato Kosir	Ministry of Culture Republic of Slovenia	QuarkXPress	Magna Matte Satin Fedrigoni Cotton Laid

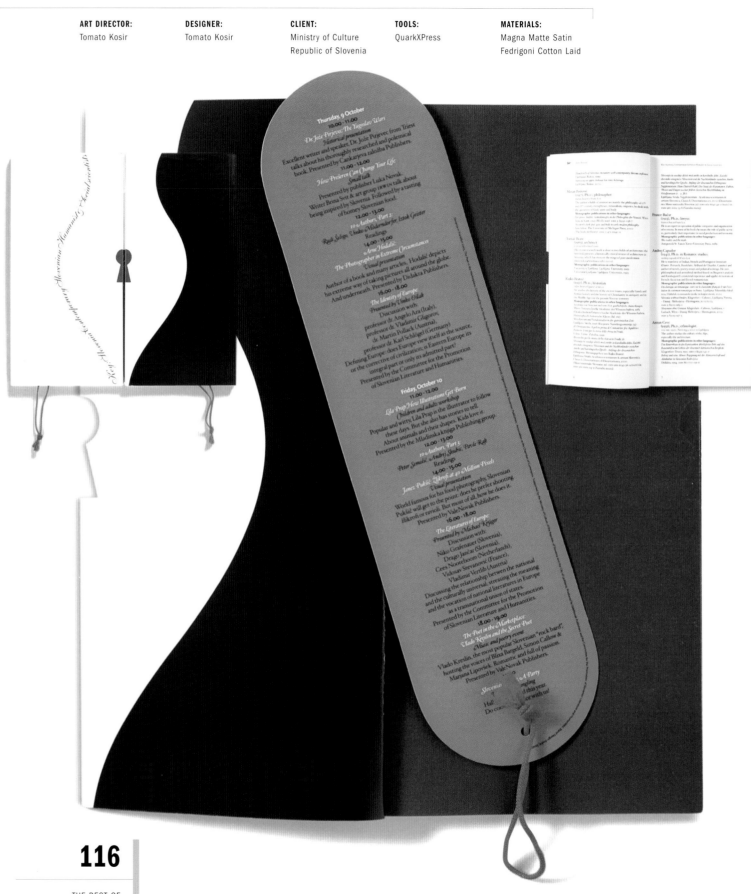

ALTERPOP

The Nature Conservancy Brochure

ART DIRECTOR:
Dorothy Remington

DESIGNERS:
Kimberly Powell
Kern Toy

CLIENT:
The Nature Conservancy

TOOLS:
Adobe InDesign

RCDP

AFDA Brochure

ART DIRECTOR:	DESIGNER:	CLIENT:	TOOLS:	MATERIALS:
Brian Palmer	Brian Palmer	AFDA	Adobe Photoshop Macromedia Freehand	Unique white 130gsm Printed 6x spot colors Kraft board (debossed) Fasson adhesive paper Wiro binding

people **and** place

technical **services**

Enesar's technical expertise lies in the physical, biological and chemical sciences and the integration of these disciplines into the analytical tools of impact assessment, mitigation and management. We have capability in spatial information systems and graphics and conduct field investigations in remote and difficult places.

We understand the engineering and commercial context and critical environmental and social interfaces of the industries in which we work: mining and minerals processing; oil and gas production; pipelines, roads, electricity generation and transmission systems; forest products, and urban development.

Enesar's technical services can be categorised into the following ten areas. Each is summarised in technical brochures downloadable from www.enesar.com.au

WATTS DESIGN

Enesar Brochure

DESIGNER:	**CLIENT:**	**TOOLS:**
Natasha Iskandar	Enesar	Adobe Photoshop
		QuarkXPress

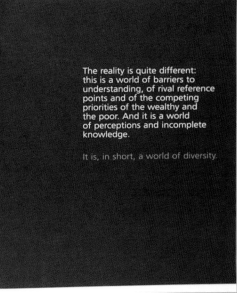

The reality is quite different: this is a world of barriers to understanding, of rival reference points and of the competing priorities of the wealthy and the poor. And it is a world of perceptions and incomplete knowledge.

It is, in short, a world of diversity.

119

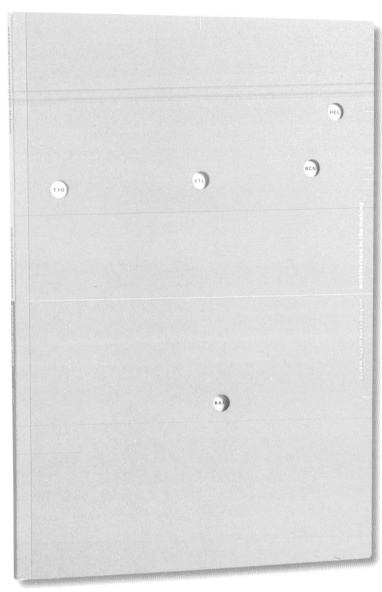

CONCRETE

School of Architecture, Washington University
in St. Louis, 2004 Bulletin

ART DIRECTOR:	DESIGNERS:	CLIENT:	TOOLS:	MATERIALS:
Jilly Simons	Jilly Simons	School of Architecture	QuarkXPress	Finch Fine
	Regan Todd	Washington University		Sappi Porcelain
		in St. Louis		

GEORGE TSCHERNY, INC.

Hurra! We Made It—Brochure

ART DIRECTOR:	DESIGNERS:	PHOTOGRAPHER:	CLIENT:	TOOLS:	MATERIALS:
Siles H. Rhodess	George Tscherny	Joseph Sinnot	School of Visual Arts	Adobe Photoshop	Centura white dull
	Matthew Cocco			QuarkXPress	white 80 lb (cover)

HAT-TRICK DESIGN

The Graduate Pioneer Programme

ART DIRECTORS:	DESIGNERS:	CLIENT:	TOOLS:	MATERIALS:
Gareth Howat	David Kimpton	Nesta	Adobe Photoshop	Naturalis
David Kimpton	Jamie Ellul		QuarkXPress	
Jim Sutherland	Mark Wheatcroft			

You'll leave The Academy with a business plan ready for investment analysis and a business-ready mindset. You'll have up to four more days of mentoring (spread over a year) and access to NESTA's online business support network.

You will also have the opportunity to present your ideas to a NESTA panel. In our pilot year, we will select twelve individuals who will receive an investment of up to £35,000 to help start up a business, mentoring for up to four years and access to a NESTA support manager.

NESNADNY + SCHWARTZ

Case Western Reserve University
Peter B. Lewis Grand Opening
Dedication Brochure

ART DIRECTORS:
Mark Schwartz
Michelle Moehler
Gregory Oznowich
Stacie Ross

DESIGNERS:
Michelle Moehler
Gregory Oznowich
Stacie Ross

CLIENT:
Case Western Reserve
University and
Weatherhead School
of Management

TOOLS:
Adobe Photoshop
Adobe Illustrator
QuarkXPress

MATERIALS:
Mohawk Option
Kromekoteplus
Benefit

A real taste of Scotland

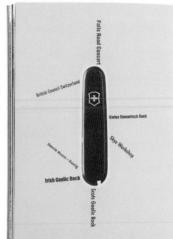

REDPATH

Moving with the Times

ART DIRECTOR:	DESIGNER:	CLIENT:	TOOLS:	MATERIALS:
Andrew Hunter	Sarah Cassells	British Council (Scotland)	Adobe Illustrator QuarkXPress	Munken Lynx 350 gsm 170 gsm

МЯСТОТО НА ЕКЗЕКУЦИЯТА

Or, translated back into English, 'A Place of Execution' by Scottish writer Val McDermid. Translated back from which language? Bulgarian. The McDermid novel, along with 'Lanark' by Alasdair Gray and 'Kiln' by William McIlvanney have all been translated into Bulgarian following the British Council's hugely successful 'Scottish Writers in Bulgaria' Literature Festival held in Sofia in October 2001.

There was a significant presence of Scottish writers at the festival – in addition to the writers mentioned above, Liz Lochhead, Irvine Welsh, Robin Robertson, David Cunningham and Martin Macquillan joined fifteen Bulgarian writers and literary critics for the three day event.

BRITISH COUNCIL
Scotland

Moving with the times

Next steppes

When Omsk Department of Education in Russia set out to develop new approaches to structuring the content of vocational education, they turned to the British Council, which facilitated a partnership between Omsk and the Scottish Qualifications Authority (SQA).

SQA has developed a flexible, modular system for qualifications that is based on core skills that are transferable between academic and vocational subjects. Education reformers in Russia want to adopt a similar system to replace their traditionally 'narrow' subject specialisations.

Since then there has been a 'snowball' effect in the development of links between the Russian educational system and Scotland, with the support of the British Council both in Russia and Scotland. Projects are currently supported in Nizhnii Novgorod and Irkutsk, as well as Omsk, drawing on Scottish experience and expertise through partnerships with the Kibble Care Centre and James Watt College, as well as with SQA.

125

Type it Write

and prepare your documents professionally

A *Voice* Project

Common sense prevails when using numerals

16 March 2003

Always use numerals for dates, or spell only the month.

16/03/03

Sometimes it's easier to spell out large numbers, especially in sentences.

One million

~~1,000,000~~

Spell out numbers under 10. For numbers 10 and over, write as numerals.

It takes nine hours, not 12.

In a series of numbers, tables or when making comparisons, it's preferable to use numerals, especially when incorporating decimal points.

$20,000 in 2002
$29,000 in 2003

US dollar	0.6782
Euro	0.5611
UK pound	0.3868
NZ dollar	1.0467

Semicolons have two common uses:

· to connect two separate, but related sentences where the joining word has been omitted

We arrived at Machu Picchu; we were immediately in awe.

· to separate items in a list where the items already contain commas.

Available in Salzburg, Austria; Rome, Italy; Santiago, Chile and Adelaide, Australia.

An ampersand means and. Use ampersands when stating some organisational names and titles, or authors in lists.

Alternative style ampersands: & & & & &

Wallbridge & Gilbert, P&A
(Dalton, Heppell & James)

VOICE
Type it Write

ART DIRECTOR:
Scott Carslake

DESIGNERS:
Scott Carslake
Anthony Deleo

CLIENT:
Voice

TOOLS:
Macromedia Freehand
QuarkXPress

RUTGERS UNIVERSITY

Rutgers Study Abroad—Recruitment Brochure

ART DIRECTOR:	DESIGNER:	CLIENT:	TOOLS:	MATERIALS:	MATERIALS:
John Van Cleaf	John Van Cleaf	Rutgers Study Abroad	Adobe Photoshop QuarkXPress	French Paper Durotone Butcher, off white 100 lb (cover)	Finch Vanilla Fine 105 lb (text)

NONPROFIT | EDUCATIONAL
INSTITUTIONAL

A PLACE FOR 21ST CENTURY SCIENCE
The Campaign for the New Academy

Nn
N is for Natural History Museum.
The Academy is one of the 10 largest
in the world.

Qq
Q is for Questions.
What would you like to know?

Uu
U is for Ulysses Butterfly,
a blue giant with a wingspan of nearly six inches.

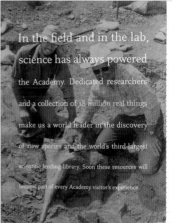

In the field and in the lab,
science has always powered
the Academy. Dedicated researchers
and a collection of 18 million real things
make us a world leader in the discovery
of new species and the world's third-largest
scientific lending library. Soon these resources will
become part of every Academy visitor's experience.

A PLACE FOR OUR BIODIVERSITY

A key participant in assessing global biodiversity, in remote
parts of the world and in our own backyards, the Academy has
helped define Earth's biodiversity "hot spots." In 25 countries,
our scientists have uncovered more than 2,000 unique
creatures and plants never before documented, putting each
into evolutionary context. Their work makes the Academy
a rare institution, with expertise encompassing the breadth
of life on Earth, from microbe to man, and a vital resource to
scientists the world over.

in decline. Less than 25 percent of U.S. elementary school
teachers have had any formal science training. Less than 20
percent of high school seniors have a good grasp of science.
And in 2000, California's 4th and 8th graders ranked last in the
country on standardized tests.

IT'S TIME A BUILDING WORTHY OF OUR MISSION

NOW WE INVITE YOU to help us transform the
Academy from a historic institution of science and education
into a 21st century engine for scientific research and literacy
— redesigned to promote discovery, learning, and collaboration,
powered by technology, "green" in spirit and function. With
innovation as our heritage, we can reinvent the California
Academy of Sciences for a new century of discovery.

ALTERPOP

California Academy of Sciences Brochure

ART DIRECTOR:
Dorothy Remington

DESIGNER:
Christopher Simmons

CLIENT:
California Academy
of Sciences

TOOLS:
Adobe Photoshop
Adobe InDesign

Oo
O is for Ornithology,
a science for those who appreciate
life on the wing.

Rr
R is for Rhinoceros, relative of the dinosaurs?
Decide for yourself at African Hall.

BUILDING ON 150 YEARS OF INNOVATION

For more than 150 years, the California
Academy of Sciences has been asking and
answering questions about our natural
world in ways that make science exciting
and meaningful to people of all ages and
cultures. While Academy scientists have
enriched our understanding of Earth's
biodiversity with their discoveries, more
than 100 million visitors have passed
through the Academy's doors, leaving
with new insight and inspiration.
The California Academy of Sciences enters the 21st century
by confronting challenges that will shape our relationship
with science for generations to come. Extinction threatens a
growing number of species. Surveys reveal that people feel
increasingly disconnected from nature. Scientific literacy is

NASSAR DESIGN

Primary School Brochure

ART DIRECTOR:	DESIGNER:	CLIENT:	TOOLS:	MATERIALS:
Nelida Nassar	Margarita Encomienda	Louise Wegmann	Adobe Photoshop	Splendorgel 340 lb
			Adobe Illustrator	grs (cover)
			QuarkXPress	Splendorgel 140 lb
				grs (text)

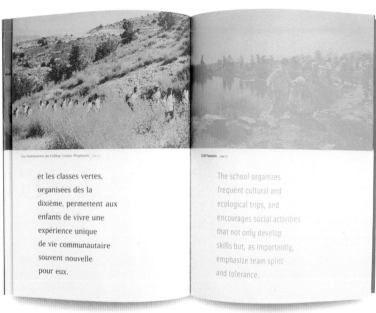

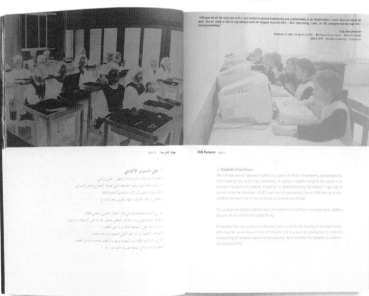

Collège Louise Wegmann

مدرسة لويز فكمان

Power the Promise **The Campaign for Planned Parenthood**

NESNADNY + SCHWARTZ

Planned Parenthood Federation of America Campaign

ART DIRECTORS:	DESIGNERS:	CLIENT:	TOOLS:	MATERIALS:
Mark Schwartz	Joyce Nesnadny	Planned Parenthood	Adobe Photoshop	Sappi
Joyce Nesnadny	Gregory Oznowich	Federation of America	Adobe Illustrator	Via
Gregory Oznowich	Stacie Ross		QuarkXPress	

power | promise

Power the Promise **The Campaign for Planned Parenthood**

power

Power the Promise The Campaign for Planned Parenthood

global

Power the Promise The Campaign for Planned Parenthood

Planned Parenthood®

www.plannedparenthood.org

Power the Prom

power

information techno

This new century bring with it exciting advances in health and learning. We all share the responsibility of ensuring that these opportunities are not out of reach for the people who need them the most.

Power the Promise **The Campaign for Planned Parenthood**

THE MAJORITY OF AMERICANS TRUSTS WOMEN TO MAKE THEIR

FREEDOM

OWN MORALLY RESPONSIBLE FAMILY PLANNING DECISIONS

WITHOUT INTERFERENCE FROM THE GOVERNMENT.

1952
Planned Parenthood Federation of America is one of the founding members of the International Planned Parenthood Federation.

1960
The U.S. Food and Drug Administration (FDA) approves the sale of oral contraceptive pills for contraception.

1967
The United Nations proclaims family planning a basic human right and establishes the UN Fund for Population Activities.

As Americans, we are taught to cherish freedom, yet the freedom to choose is at risk. Government is choking family planning funding and censoring sex education. Elected officials disregard the views of the pro-choice majority, who believes reproductive choice belongs to a woman, her doctor, and her conscience, not politicians or government. Roe v. Wade is a fragile line of defense. Vocal, well-funded, disproportionately powerful anti-choice hardliners hold sway over the debate.

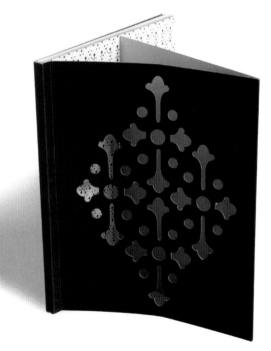

INARIA

Ball Programme 2003

ART DIRECTOR:
Andrew Thomas

DESIGNERS:
Andrew Thomas
Debora Berardi

CLIENT:
Anti-Slavery
International

TOOLS:
Adobe Photoshop
Adobe Illustrator
QuarkXPress

MATERIALS:
Colourplan
Hello matt

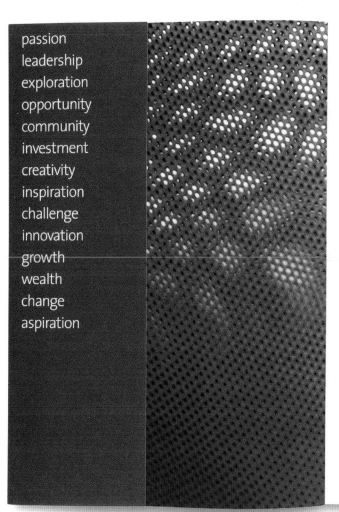

passion
leadership
exploration
opportunity
community
investment
creativity
inspiration
challenge
innovation
growth
wealth
change
aspiration

Welcome to 'knowledge', a celebration of RMIT University's passion and commitment to make a difference through education, research and innovation.

PERKS DESIGN PARTNERS

RMIT Capabilities Document

ART DIRECTOR:	DESIGNER:	CLIENT:	TOOLS:	MATERIALS:
Chris Perks	Maurice Lai	RMIT University	QuarkXPress	Raleigh Look four-color process plus one PMS clear foil stamping on cover

2002

LES TROPHÉES ÉTUDIANTS
DE L'INNOVATION ALIMENTAIRE

APÉRIMEX

Étudiants :
Fleury Bougaud
Aurélie Fillet
Marion Forestier
M.-Caroline Guggenberg
Christine Izou
Azoul Lakrao
Matthieu Long
Marc Manzoni
Meriam Mejjora
Holder Mendes Barbosa
Enseignants :
Jean-Claude Gretin
Pascal Degraeve

Positionné sur le marché en pleine croissance des produits de snac-king exotiques, le Mole Poblano est un plat traditionnel mexicain. Des morceaux de poulet accompagnés d'une savoureuse sauce épicée sont entourés de lanières de tortillas de maïs. La sauce associe des épices à la douce amertume du chocolat qui lui confèrent des caractéristiques organoleptiques remarquables.
Présentées sous forme de kit en rayon frais, les bouchées de poulet se conservent 21 jours au réfrigérateur et ne nécessitent que dix minutes de préparation. Le kit se compose d'un sachet contenant les bouchées de poulet ensaucées, d'un sachet contenant les lanières de tortillas ainsi que d'un sachet de quinze piques. Réchauffables en trente secondes au four micro-ondes ou en cinq minutes dans un four chaud (180 °C), les bouchées de Mole Poblano ou *Apérimex* se dégustent aussi bien en apéritif que pour un petit creux.
Les *Apérimex* sont nés de la volonté d'offrir aux consommateurs un produit original alliant toute l'authenticité du Mexique mise au goût européen. Issus d'un mélange savant entre la cuisine traditionnelle mexicaine et l'innovation (présentation sous forme d'un kit), les *Apérimex* surprendront vos amis et apporteront de la convivialité à vos soirées.

I.U.T.A LYON 1
IUT A LYON 1
Rue Henri-de-Boissieu
01060 Bourg-en-Bresse
Cedex 09
Tel : 04 74 45 52 52
Fax : 04 74 45 52 53

16　　17

ANNE-LISE DERMENGHEM
Student Contest Brochure

ART DIRECTOR:	DESIGNER:	CLIENT:	PRINTER:	TOOLS:	MATERIALS:
Anne-Lise Dermenghem	Anne-Lise Dermenghem	Actia	Amigon	Adobe Photoshop	Old Mill, Feutricoti
				Adobe Illustrator	
				QuarkXPress	
				pOnoir	

VITARÉCRÉ

Étudiants :
Sophie Delcour
Lucie Lamoureux
Anne-Sophie Le Corre
Karine Von Meiss
Enseignants :
Pascal Barillon
Franck Daros
Anne Desruineaux
Annie Lambert
Jean-Louis Lambert

Initier les enfants aux plaisirs des légumes de façon ludique et attractive, tel est l'enjeu de *Vitarécré*.

Vitarécré est un moyen innovant de faire manger des légumes aux enfants de six à douze ans. Ce snack extrudé, contenant des légumes aux saveurs prononcées, fraix, plaira aux enfants par sa croustillance et ses aspects ludiques.

Dans un souci de rééquilibre pour le grignotage des enfants, *Vitarécré* contient trois fois moins de matières grasses que les goûters classiques. Il contribue ainsi à une bonne hygiène de vie alimentaire grâce à tous les bienfaits des légumes. *Vitarécré* s'inscrit en effet dans les tendances actuelles de retour aux sources et de souci d'équilibre nutritionnel.

Vitarécré se présente en lots de quatre sachets de 25 g pour caler toutes les faims des enfants. Il se décline en plusieurs saveurs : carotte, brocoli, tomate, poivron rouge, tomate-poivron rouge, épinard. Avec son format pocket très résistant et à fond plat, *Vitarécré* peut se glisser dans tous les sacs et en toutes occasions.

Positionné sur le marché du snacking salé en plein essor, on pourra trouver *Vitarécré* en grandes et moyennes surfaces dans le rayon des produits salés pour l'apéritif.

ENITIAA
ÉCOLE NATIONALE D'INGÉNIEURS
DES TECHNIQUES DES INDUSTRIES
AGRICOLES ET ALIMENTAIRES
Rue de la Géraudière
B.P. 82225
44322 Nantes Cedex 3
Tel : 02 51 78 54 54
Fax : 02 51 78 54 55

40　　41

DANIELLE FOUSHÉE DESIGN

4 Days of Fashion Announcement
and FIDM Scholarship Brochure

ART DIRECTOR:	DESIGNER:	CLIENT:	TOOLS:	MATERIALS:
Danielle Foushée	Danielle Foushée	The Fashion Institute of Design & Merchandising	Adobe Photoshop Adobe Illustrator	Magna Dull 100 lb (cover)

135

NONPROFIT | EDUCATIONAL
INSTITUTIONAL

re-

think

Where would we be without forests? How would their absence affect everyday life? What would happen to our watersheds, wildlife, climate, and the livelihoods of all those who depend on forests? Forests are a fundamental component of our natural environment and national economy. They support a $74-billion forest industry that employs 361,000 Canadians, and serve as a backdrop to a huge tourism industry. At the Natural Sciences and Engineering Research Council of Canada (NSERC), we recognize the vital importance of this renewable resource and the immense challenges that face those who seek to understand and offer solutions to ensure the future health of the forest. We put our confidence in those who ask the difficult questions. We believe that knowledge – the kind that comes from advanced research by talented well-trained experts – is essential to informed decision-making. NSERC's role is to make investments in people, discovery and innovation for the benefit of all Canadians.

Natural Sciences and Engineering Research Council of Canada   Conseil de recherches en sciences naturelles et en génie du Canada

STORM VISUAL COMMUNICATIONS INC.

Forestry Brochure

ART DIRECTOR:	DESIGNER:	CLIENT:	TOOLS:
Chantal Lancaster	Chantal Lancaster	Natural Sciences and Engineering Research Council of Canada	Adobe Photoshop Adobe Illustrator QuarkXPress

reward: In addition to moderating climate, preventing soil erosion, improving air and water quality, and providing habitat for countless plants and animals, our forests sustain the economies of hundreds of communities across Canada.

seeds of change

The genetic resources of forest trees are an important economic and ecological resource in Canada and gene conservation is accomplished through the maintenance of large populations of trees in reserves, such as parks and ecological areas. However the assumption that "local seed is best" is based on the idea that the offspring that are planted locally will experience a similar climate to that faced by their parents, grandparents and more distant ancestors. We now know that this is increasingly not the case and if global climate change results in even a small decline in tree growth rates, the effect on long-term wood and fibre production could be substantial. It could mean a reduction of the total amount of timber grown and available to the forest industry, as well as a reduction of the net amount of carbon fixed in Canada's forests.

British Columbia plants more than 200 million seedlings annually. Will these trees be able to adapt to a changing climate? Dr. Aitken is exploring these questions and looking for means of mitigating the effects of climate change. Her research team plans to mix seed from different populations and evaluate the ability of conservation

CHAQUE MINUTE DE CHAQUE HEURE CHACUN NOUS TIENT À CŒUR

La Campagne Héritage de La Fondation de l'Hôpital d'Ottawa

STORM VISUAL COMMUNICATIONS INC.

Legacy Brochure

ART DIRECTOR:	DESIGNER:	CLIENT:	TOOLS:	MATERIALS:
Robert Smith	Robert Smith	Ottawa Hospital Foundation	Adobe Photoshop Adobe Illustrator QuarkXPress	Uses the same stickers and fasteners as hospital charts

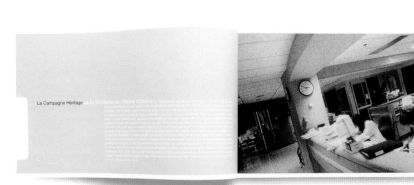

MIRKO ILIĆ CORP.

Massachusetts Lesbian & Gay Bar
Association Brochures

ART DIRECTOR:	CLIENT:	TOOLS:
Mirko Ilić	Massachusetts Lesbian & Gay Bar Association	QuarkXPress

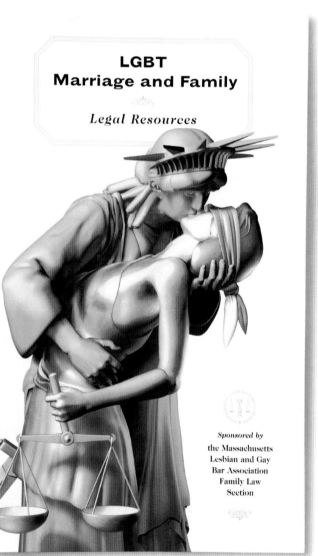

DESIGNER:	CLIENT:	TOOLS:	MATERIALS:
Melissa Wehrman	AIGA Boston	Adobe Photoshop Adobe Illustrator QuarkXPress	Finch Smooth bright white 80 lb cover

AIGA's purpose is to further excellence in design as a broadly defined discipline, strategic tool for business and cultural force.

PARTICIPATE

AIGA is a professional association committed to stimulating thinking about design through the exchange of ideas and information, the encouragement of critical analysis and research and the advancement of education and ethical practice.

Join the largest network of designers in the country because issues that matter definitely are professional to designers in designers, advocating the value of design among business communities, governments, studios, and the public, and developing standards for professional practice.

BOSTON.AIGA.ORG

Expanding Your Profession
Have a voice in the national dialogue on the role of design. From participating in local events to exploring professional challenges, you'll be playing a vital part in protecting, promoting, and advancing the power of design.

Supporting Your Career
How much should I be earning? How do I handle this project? Where can I find a job? A partner? An idea? AIGA supports members with career and business building resources that inspire and motivate.

Advancing Your Talent
Expand your skills through local design events, workshops, seminars, and classes.

Building Connections
Be part of a larger community with your AIGA membership. Whether nationally or locally, AIGA helps you build relationships with colleagues who will interest you, support you, and challenge you.

Saving You Money
AIGA members receive discounts on local and national AIGA events, calls for entry, design publications, business support services, and more.

Becoming A Member
To join, sign up online at www.aiga.org/join or fax/mail the application. If you have questions, please call the national office at 1 800 548 1634 or the Boston hotline at 781 446 9082.

For a complete list of benefits that our members are currently enjoying, visit boston.aiga.org.

XHILARATE
OMMUNICATE
MOTIVATE
CREATE
STIMULATE
DUCATE
FABRICATE
ACTIVATE

139

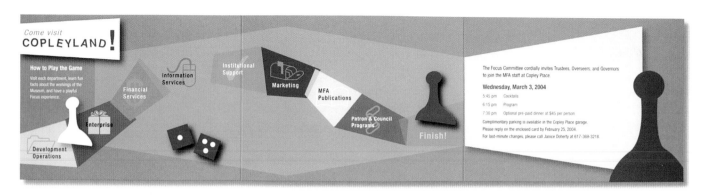

MUSEUM OF FINE ARTS, BOSTON
Copley Land Event Brochure

ART DIRECTOR:	DESIGNER:	CLIENT:	TOOLS:	MATERIALS:
Janet O'Donoghue	Julie Grønneberg Shulman	Museum of Fine Arts, Boston	Adobe Photoshop QuarkXPress	Finch Fine uncoated 100 lb (cover)

HAMMERPRESS

Young Architects Forum

ART DIRECTOR:	DESIGNER:	CLIENT:	TOOLS:	MATERIALS:
Brady Vest	Brady Vest	Young Architects Forum	letterpress	chipboard

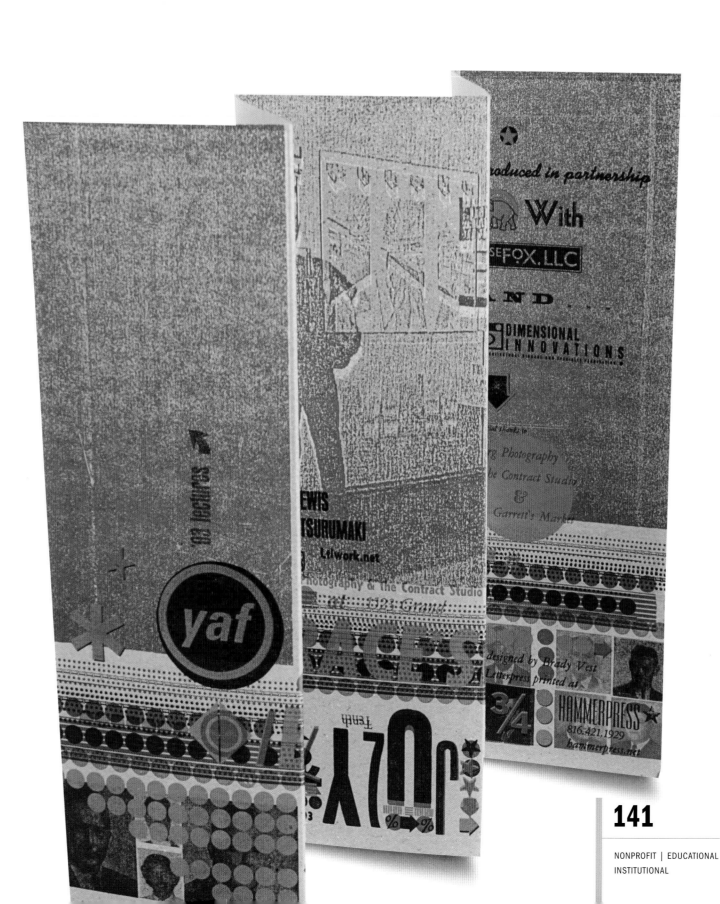

SELF-PROMOTIONAL

INEDEBOUTONSPAULAKELLYDESIGNBNIMARCHITECTSGRETEMANGROUPHANGER18CREATIVEG
PERKSDESIGNPARTNERS SOPHIEBARTHO+ASSOCIATESIRONDESIGN
GNDESIGNAHEADSAGMEISTERINCINSIGHTDESIGNCOMMUNICATIONSVINE360
ECHTERWORLDWIDEPARTNERS KOLEGRAMNESNADNY+SCHWARTZKBDAWEYMOUTHDESIGNZI
GN PENTAGRAMDESIGNTHEDAVEANDALEXSHOWHORNALLANDERSONDESIGN
SINCWATTSDESIGNMAGMA[BÜROFÜRGESTALTUNG]&CHRISTIANERNST DO
GNBAUMANN&BAUMANNHIPPOSTUDIO ÓBLACKLETTERDESIGN PATH HATTRI
USINEDEBOUTONSPAULAKELLYDESIGNBNIMARCHITECTSGRETEMANGROUP ANGER CRE
OUPTRACY DESIGN COMMUNICATIONS PERKSDESIGNPARTNERSSOPHIEBARTHO+ASSOCIATESIR
GNCDTDESIGN DESIGNAHEAD SAGMEISTERINC VINE360
WAECHTER&WAECHTERWORLDWIDEPARTNERSKOLEGRAMNESNADNY+SCHWARTZ KBD
ZIGZAGDESIGNLIQUIDAGENCYINC PENTAGRAMDESIGN THEDAVEANDALEXSHOW
USINEDEBOUTONSPAULAKELLYDESIGNBNIMARCHITECTSGRETEMANGROUPHANGER
VEGROUPTRACYDESIGNCOMMUNICATIONSPERKSDESIGNPARTNERS SOPHIEBARTHO+ASSOCIA

USINE DE BOUTONS
CARILLON

ART DIRECTOR:	DESIGNERS:	CLIENT:	TOOLS:
Chiara Grandesso	Chiara Grandesso	REPLAY & SONS	Adobe Illustrator
	Lionello Borean		

144

TABLE TOP ICONS:

Novelty
Salt and
Pepper
Shakers

The Michael Hall and Pat Glascock Collection

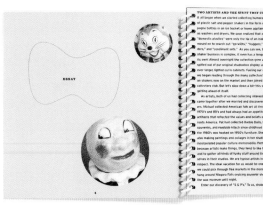

PAULA KELLY DESIGN

Gallery Exhibit Catalog for Collection
of Vintage Salt and Pepper Shakers

ART DIRECTOR:	DESIGNER:	CLIENT:	TOOLS:	MATERIALS:
Paula Kelly	Paula Kelly	Greenwich House Pottery	Adobe Illustrator	Utopia Two
		Jane Hatsook Gallery	QuarkXPress	(cover and text)

Huggers, nodders, nesters and something called a "go-with" Shaker pairs orchestrated as narratives and ensembles

**PAIRING CONCEPTS/
SERIES CONCEPTS**

10

PAIRING CONCEPTS—*row 1:* MOTHER AND BABY POLAR BEAR nester set 1940's (*U.S.A. Ceramic Arts Studio*), SEA SHELLS condiment set on tray 1930's (*England*). DIVER WITH SHARKS cruet set 1940's (*Japan*). *row 2:* INDIAN COUPLE IN A DRUM nodder set 1960's (*Japan*). PAIR OF CATS luster ware one-piece set 1930's (*Japan*). MARTINI AND ASPIRIN go-with set 1950's (*U.S.A., B. Standish*), YOUNG BRIDE AND GROOM/OLD MARRIED COUPLE turn-a-bout set 1950's (*Japan*). *row 3:* ELEPHANTS IN A SWING swinger set 1940's (*Japan*), LOVE BUGS hugger set 1950's (*U.S.A., Regal China*), TOMATO MAN IN TOP HAT stacker set 1940's (*Japan*). SERIES CONCEPTS—*row 4:* HOME AND OFFICE PEOPLE: Pan Head Lads, Iron Head Ladies, Telephone Head Girls, Typewriter Head Boys/ *complete series contains 12 sets* 1950's (*Japan*). ● *opposite page:* SPOON PROPOSING TO FORK, go-with, 1950's (*Japan*)

11

What if you could **lead** the region or the **nation** toward a **new vision** for **industry?**

add value to the community.

increase productivity.

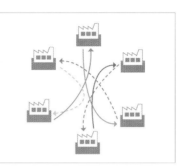

What if you could **turn** your **waste** into a **product** that had **market value?**

BNIM ARCHITECTS

By-Product Synergy Brochure

ART DIRECTOR:	DESIGNER:	CLIENT:	TOOLS:	MATERIALS:
Zack Shubkagel	Zack Shubkagel	Kansas City Regional By-Product Synergy Initiative	Adobe InDesign Adobe Illustrator	Benefit (cover) Mohawk (text)

147

TOMATO KOSIR

Flipbook Calendar "Celoletni Listavec"

ART DIRECTOR:	DESIGNER:	CLIENT:	TOOLS:	MATERIALS:
Tomato Kosir	Tomato Kosir	Youth Service Center, Kranj	Adobe Illustrator	Magna matt

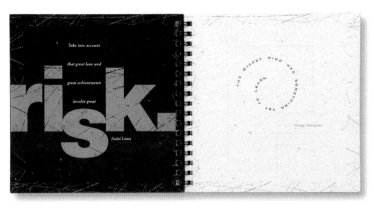

GRETEMAN GROUP

Read & Reap

ART DIRECTOR:	**DESIGNERS:**	**ILLUSTRATOR:**	**CLIENT:**	**TOOLS:**
Sonia Greteman	James Strange	James Strange	Greteman Group	Macromedia Freehand
CREATIVE DIRECTOR:	Craig Tomson	**COPYWRITERS:**		
Sonia Greteman		Sonia Greteman		
		Raleigh Drennon		

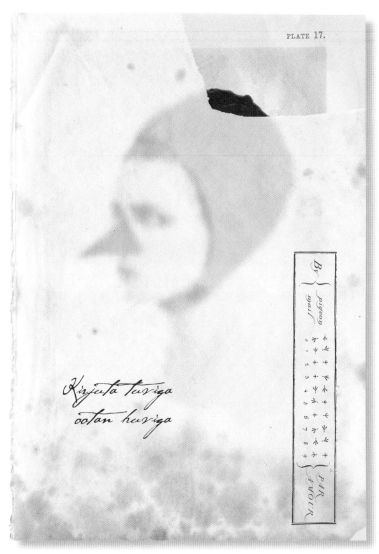

RUTH HUIMERIND

The Retro-Flavour Christmas Booklet
of the Paper Company

ART DIRECTOR:	DESIGNER:	CLIENT:	TOOLS:	MATERIALS:
Ruth Huimerind	Jyri Loun	Map Eesti	Macromedia Freehand	Century Acquarello
				Stucco Gesso

150

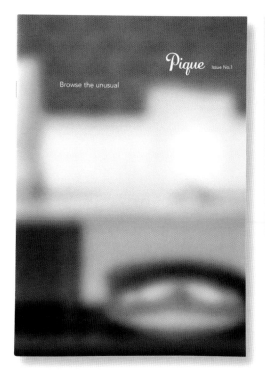

BBK STUDIO

Pique Catalog

ART DIRECTORS:	DESIGNER:	CLIENT:	TOOLS:	MATERIALS:
Yang Kim	Michele Chartier	Pique	Adobe Photoshop	Monadnock Astrolight
Michele Chartier			Adobe Illustrator	Super smooth
			QuarkXPress	

HANGAR 18 CREATIVE GROUP

Starbright Paper Brochure

DESIGNER:	CLIENT:	TOOLS:	MATERIALS:
Sean Carter	Unisource Paper	QuarkXPress	Starbright Paper

★ Job Opportunities

Cerner's comprehensive six-month sales training program offers an opportunity to learn and apply Cerner's approach to managing existing client relationships, developing marketing programs, and selling directly to clients. Learn about today's health care environment and join the front lines in Cerner's drive to transform it; train in the Cerner sales process and complex consultative sales techniques. The program includes mentoring by successful Cerner sales associates and is designed to teach solution selling skills, sales lead development and tracking, market positioning, and financial ROI modeling. The program is open to new college graduates, as well as candidates who possess one to two years of prior work experience.

persons, kno
iate time and
h outcome.

talent & passion

TRACY DESIGN COMMUNICATIONS
Recruitment Desk/Brochure

ART DIRECTOR:	**DESIGNER:**	**CLIENT:**	**TOOLS:**	**MATERIALS:**
Jan Tracy	Patrick Simon	Cerner Corp.	Adobe Photoshop	Utopia Premium
			Adobe Illustrator	
			QuarkXPress	

PerksDesignPartners

PERKS DESIGN PARTNERS
Perks Design Partners, Self Promotion

ART DIRECTOR: Chris Perks

DESIGNER: Maurice Lai

CLIENT: Perks Design Partners

TOOLS: Adobe Photoshop Adobe InDesign

MATERIALS: Oxford Smoke gloss foil stamp (slipcase) Parilux and Superfine Ultra Smooth (brochure)

SOPHIE BARTHO + ASSOCIATES
Moirs Paper 2004 Calendar

ART DIRECTOR:
Michèle Alexander

DESIGNER:
Lynette Ee
WRITERS:
SBA

ILLUSTRATORS:
Michèle Alexander
Lynette Ee

CLIENT:
Moirs Paper

TOOLS:
Adobe Photoshop
Adobe Illustrator
QuarkXPress
pen and paper

MATERIALS:
Curious Metallic Ionized
Antique
Galerie Image
Envirocare
Taktik

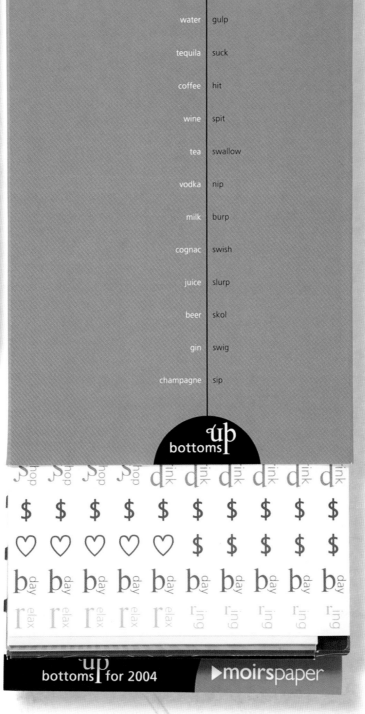

water   gulp

tequila   suck

coffee   hit

wine   spit

tea   swallow

vodka   nip

milk   burp

cognac   swish

juice   slurp

beer   skol

gin   swig

champagne   sip

bottoms up

YOU ALWAYS FEEL
BUFFALO THEORY
it's logical
PRODUCT OF BEER LOVING
SMARTER AFTER A FEW BEERS

october
november
december

up
bottoms for 2004   ►moirspaper

up
bottoms for 2004   ►moirspaper

IRON DESIGN
Mini Portfolio

ART DIRECTOR:	DESIGNERS:	CLIENT:	TOOLS:	MATERIALS:
Todd Edmonds	Todd Edmonds Xanthe Matychak	Iron Design	Adobe Illustrator	Matchbook

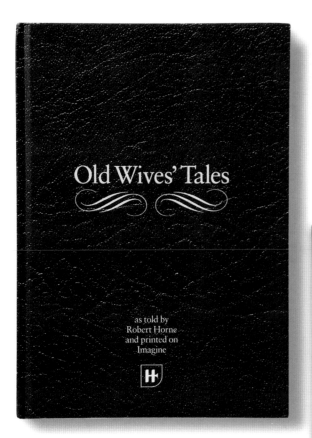

CDT DESIGN
Promotional Brochure

ART DIRECTOR:	DESIGNER:	CLIENT:	TOOLS:	MATERIALS:
Christian Altmann	Sophie Paynter	Robert Horne Group	Adobe Photoshop Adobe Illustrator, QuarkXPress	Imagine

DESIGN AHEAD

Image Brochure for a Design Agency

ART DIRECTOR:	DESIGNER:	CLIENT:	TOOLS:	MATERIALS:
Axel Voss	Axel Voss	Design Ahead	Adobe Photoshop	four-color plus copper
			Macromedia Freehand	metallic embossing
				on cover
				three books bookbound
				in slipcase

USINE DE BOUTONS
Self-Promotion

ART DIRECTOR:	DESIGNER:	CLIENT:	TOOLS:	MATERIALS:
Lionello Borean	Lionello Borean	Usine de Boutons	Adobe Illustrator	Fedrigoni GSK Paper

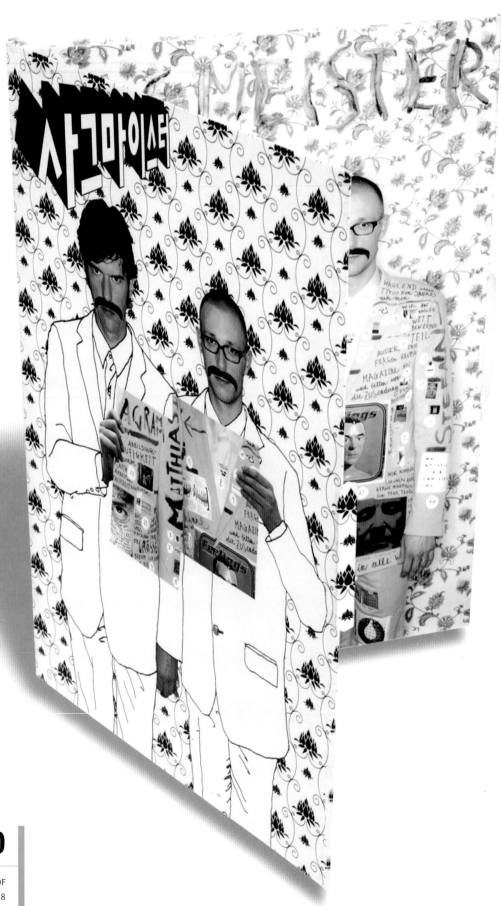

SAGMEISTER INC.
Zumtobel Annual Report

ART DIRECTOR	DESIGNERS	CLIENT	TOOLS	MATERIALS
Stefan Sagmeister	Stefan Sagmeister Matthias Ernstberger	Zumtobel	Adobe Photoshop QuarkXPress	Molded relief sculpture

161

DUFFY SINGAPORE

A Photographer's Self-Promotion Brochure

ART DIRECTOR:	DESIGNER:	CLIENT:	TOOLS:	MATERIALS:
Christoper Lee	Christoper Lee	Wizards of Light	Macromedia Freehand	Artcard
				Art Paper

162

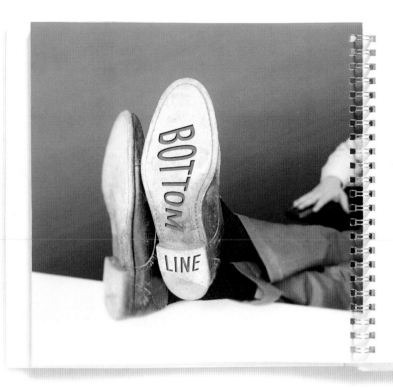

Put your feet up, this building isn't going anywhere.

Our designs raise the bar on bottom lines. We employ strategies that increase energy efficiency, flexibility, and promote durability – which will lower operating costs, and lengthen the life of your building. We design buildings that can be sustained and maintained for 100 years and beyond.

BNIM ARCHITECTS

Brand Architecture Brochure

ART DIRECTOR:	DESIGNER:	CLIENT:	TOOLS:	MATERIALS:
Zack Shubkagel	Zack Shubkagel	Bernstein-Rein Advertising	Adobe InDesign Adobe Illustrator Adobe Photoshop	French Paper Muscletone Vellum cover Mohawk (text) letterpress

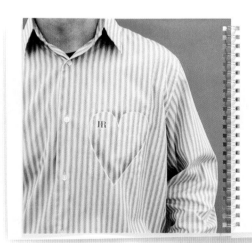

We want to tailor a home for your family at Bernstein-Rein for generations to come.

Employees are at the heart of your business. To attract and retain great talent you need a world-class environment.

BNIM has extensive experience in creating work-places that engage through collaborative spaces and inspire through health and comfort. These are places where employees control their environment and can share ideas. Our designs are proven to increase human health and productivity, which in turn will improve your bottom line. It's the people that make the difference.

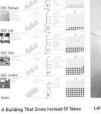

High Performance Building

Higher Performance. Lower Cost

By utilizing high performance strategies, BNIM was able to design the School of Nursing for the University of Texas Health Science Center Houston to utilize only 45% of the total energy that a conventional building of this type would use. That, of course, means significant savings in the annual operating budget for the entire life of the building with only a minimal increase in initial costs.

A Building That Gives Instead Of Takes

The Sustainability Report & Matrix was the BNIM design team's response to setting sustainability goals for the David & Lucile Packard Foundation in Los Altos, California. Design in the third millennium will require a more holistic understanding of energy conservation, consumption, generation and cost. This tool explores the financial cost of carrying through on energy and resource conscious strategies and the environmental and societal costs of not doing so.

Let The Sunshine In

Our practice is predicated on alignment with our client's values. Through close client participation and in-depth research of your workplace, we establish a lot of issues important to the success of the project. We look at variables that emphasize the bottom line while promoting users' satisfaction. A successful project embraces ideas such as flexibility, indoor air quality, daylighting, energy-efficient systems and smart technologies, future growth and technological changes in a holistic, inclusive approach.

163

REAP WHAT YOU SOW

INSIGHT DESIGN COMMUNICATIONS

Eric Fisher Salon Mission Brochure

ART DIRECTOR:	DESIGNER:	CLIENT:	TOOLS:	MATERIALS:
Tracy Holdeman	Lea Carmichael	Eric Fisher Salon	Macromedia Freehand	Wausau Royal Fiber smooth white

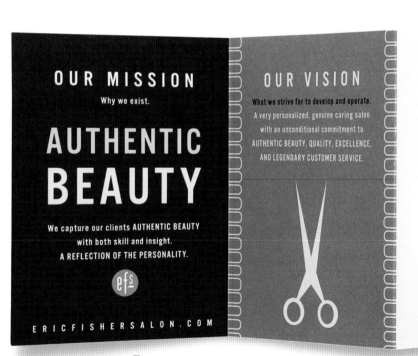

OUR MISSION

Why we exist.

AUTHENTIC BEAUTY

We capture our clients AUTHENTIC BEAUTY with both skill and insight. A REFLECTION OF THE PERSONALITY.

ericfishersalon.com

OUR VISION

What we strive for to develop and operate. A very personalized, genuine caring salon with an unconditional commitment to AUTHENTIC BEAUTY, QUALITY, EXCELLENCE, AND LEGENDARY CUSTOMER SERVICE.

OUR CORE VALUES

What we feel is important.

POSITIVITY
AUTHENTICITY
TECHNICAL EXPERTISE
LEGENDARY SERVICE
WOWING
GREAT VALUE
RELIABILITY

OUR STRATEGY

To measure how our execution we have five targets. FULFILLMENT IS SUCCESS.

90% PRODUCTION
65% RETENTION
20% PRODUCTS (S10 AVERAGE)
"PLUS" ADD ON SERVICES
70% PREBOOK

164

TRACY DESIGN COMMUNICATIONS

DDM Morris Photography Promotional

ART DIRECTOR:	DESIGNERS:	CLIENT:	TOOLS:
Jan Tracy	Tony Magliano	David Morris	Adobe Photoshop
	Rachel Karaca		Adobe Illustrator
			QuarkXPress

VINE360

VINE360 Brochure

DESIGNER:	**CLIENT:**	**TOOLS:**	**MATERIALS:**
Joy MacDonald	VINE360	Adobe Photoshop	5inch.com CD
		Adobe Illustrator	silver stardream
			inkjet cardstock
			for individual
			customization

LOGOSBRANDS

Self-Promotion Brochure

ART DIRECTOR:	DESIGNERS:	CLIENT:	TOOLS:	MATERIALS:
Franca DiNardo	Sunny Chan	Logosbrands	Adobe Photoshop	Utopia Premium One-X
	Ali Khan		Adobe Illustrator	Suede
			QuarkXPress	

WAECHTER & WAECHTER WORLDWIDE PARTNERS

Christmas Book

ART DIRECTOR:
Lothar Schmid

CREATIVE DIRECTOR:
Ulrich Schmitz

TOOLS:
Adobe Photoshop
Adobe Illustrator
QuarkXPress

Die Reise zum Elefanten

Wächter & Wächter | Worldwide Partners

Die Reise zum Elefanten

Ein Märchen.
In allen Farben gemalt von:

STEFLI

Die Gelehrten begannen heftig zu streiten. Welcher hatte nun
das richtige Tier untersucht? Hatten die Gastgeber in dem fernen
Land sie hinters Licht geführt? Wollte man ihnen das edle Wesen
doch nicht zeigen? Oder handelte es sich bei dem Elefanten gar
um eine Legende?

Seltsamerweise zeigte sich der König von dieser hitzigen Diskus-
sion wenig beeindruckt, was die Gelehrten noch mehr verunsi-
cherte. Der weise König blieb ganz ruhig und sagte: „Ich bin
enttäuscht von meinen Gelehrten, den weisesten Menschen meines
Königreiches. Der Grund für dieses Missverständnis ist nicht eure

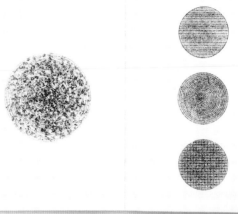

JÉRÔME**FORTIN**

KOLEGRAM
Art Exhibit Brochure

DESIGNER:	CLIENT:	TOOLS:	MATERIALS:
Jean-François Plante	Pierre-François Ouellette	Adobe Photoshop	Sappi
	Art Contemporain	QuarkXPress	Horizon

De toute évidence, l'art est pour Jérôme Fortin une activité qu'il pratique sans modération, avec une habileté qui confine à la presti-digitation. ● Dans son jeu sans fin avec les matériaux, l'arrivée des estampes s'avère inattendue; en plus, elles renouvellent le genre. Dès l'abord, elles intriguent : on s'interroge sur la technique utilisée. Ce sont de simples feuilles de papier imprimé, tirées en général d'un seul livre, découpées de bout en bout et collées sur un carton rond. ● Tout en affichant une relative uniformité visuelle, elles ont chacune leur personnalité. Il y a là une recherche étonnante dans la déclinaison des motifs, ce que les musiciens appellent des variations sur un thème. Sans jamais se lasser ou être lassant, Jérôme a exploré toute une gamme de textures, d'agencements qui évoquent des dessins aztèques ou incas, des écritures très anciennes, des végétaux ou des tissus; la liste des associations pourrait être longue car les allusions sont fines. ● Devant nos yeux, un bouquet de nuances grises, blanches et noires. Estompée ou nette, la bande explore les infinies variétés de ces tons et invite le regard à la suivre dans ses méandres. Et pourtant, les objets qui ont servi de *plaques*, les matrices, sont aussi fascinantes que les estampes. Leur léger relief, leur couleur les distinguent et en font des œuvres à part entière. À vrai dire, l'habileté joue un rôle important dans la production d'une oeuvre, mais il y a aussi le travail... ● Art, for Jérôme Fortin, is quite obviously an activity to which he devotes unstinting practice; and he does it with skillfulness that verges on magic. In his endless play with materials, printmaking in Fortin's work is unexpected; his prints, moreover, renew the genre. From the outset, they intrigue us: we wonder about the underlying technique. Simple sheets of printed paper, generally taken from a single book, cut end-to-end and glued onto a round cardboard. ● While relatively uniform visually, they each have a personality. Here is an astounding investigation into variations on some motifs — variations on a theme, as musicians say. Tirelessly, though never tiring, Jérôme explores a whole range of textures, constructions evocative of Aztec or Inca drawings, of ancient writings, of plant or fabric. One can draw up a long list of associations, for the allusions are intricate. ● Before our eyes, a bouquet of nuances: greys, whites, blacks. Whether blurred or sharp, the series explores countless varieties of these hues, inviting our gaze to follow its meandering course. And yet, the objects that served as *plates*, the moulds, are as fascinating as the prints themselves. Distinguished by their colour and low relief, they are works in their own right. In truth, while dexterity plays an important role in the production of an art work, time and effort are also a factor... **PASCALE BEAUDET**

169

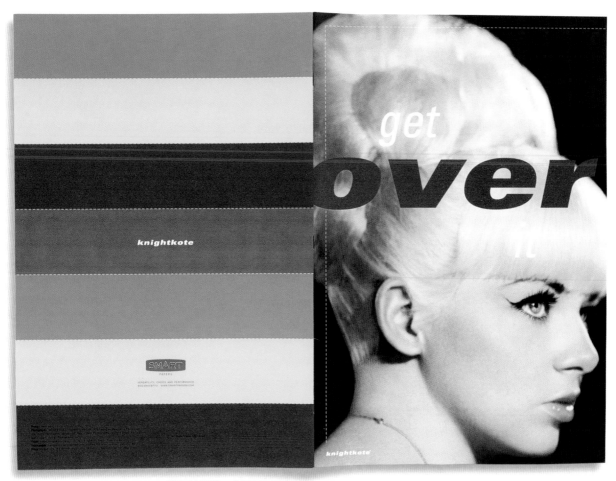

NESNADNY + SCHWARTZ
SMART Knightkote Brochure

ART DIRECTORS:	DESIGNERS:	CLIENT:	TOOLS:	MATERIALS:
Mark Schwartz	Michelle Moehler	SMART Papers	Adobe Photoshop	SMART Knightkote
Joyce Nesnadny			Adobe Illustrator	
Michelle Moehler			QuarkXPress	

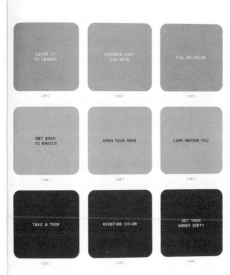

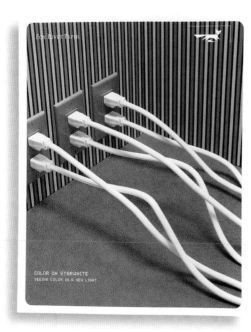

KBDA

Fox River: Color on Starwhite

ART DIRECTOR:	DESIGNER:	CLIENT:	TOOLS:	MATERIALS:
Kim Baer	Jamie Diersing	Fox River Paper Company	Adobe Photoshop Adobe Illustrator QuarkXPress	Fox River Starwhite Tiara Starwhite Archiva Starwhite Sirius in various weights and finishes

WEYMOUTH DESIGN

Weymouth Design Hands-On Self-Promotional

ART DIRECTOR:	DESIGNERS:	ILLUSTRATOR:	TOOLS:	MATERIALS:
Michael Weymouth	Bob Kellerman	Copley Pharmaceutical	Adobe Photoshop	Mohawk Navajo (text) 100 lb
	Chris Korbey	Jeffrey Decoster	Adobe Illustrator	Glama Natural Clear 29 lb
	WRITER:	CYRK	QuarkXPress	case-bound book
	Jean Gogolin	Mark S. Fisher		
	PHOTOGRAPHER:			
	Michael Weymouth			

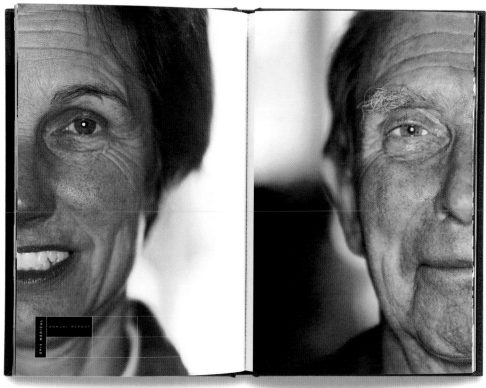

ZIGZAG DESIGN
Zigzag Design Promo Piece

ART DIRECTOR:	DESIGNER:	CLIENT:	TOOLS:	MATERIALS:
Rachel Karaca	Rachel Karaca	Zigzag Design	Adobe Photoshop Adobe Illustrator	French Speckletone Rubber

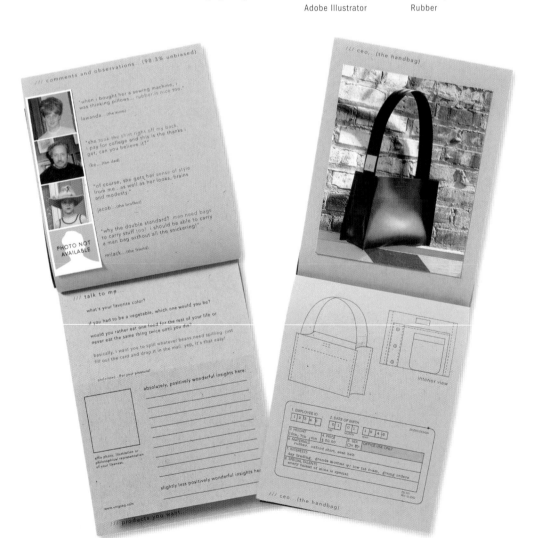

LIQUID AGENCY INC.

IN (Spring 03) Internal Brochure

ART DIRECTOR:	DESIGNER:	CLIENT:	TOOLS:
Joshua Swanbeck	Charlotte Jones	Liquid Agency Inc.	Adobe Photoshop
			Adobe Illustrator
			QuarkXPress

PAULA KELLY DESIGN

Micro Pocket Portfolio

ART DIRECTOR:	DESIGNER:	CLIENT:	TOOLS:	MATERIALS:
Paula Kelly	Paula Kelly	Paula Kelly Design/NYC	QuarkXPress	Scheufelen PhoeniXmotion 100 lb silk (text)

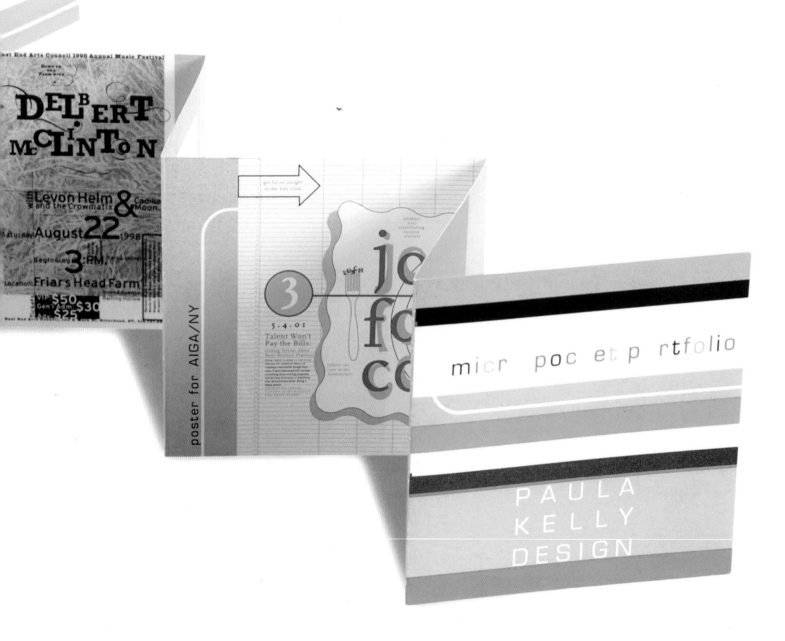

Some pairs bring out the best in each other. When the synergy is right, they complement each other's strengths, offer timely support, and make everything better and more interesting. Without Tonto, the Lone Ranger would be just a masked man lost in his tracks. Without Rudolph, Santa would still be stranded at the North Pole. Without jelly, peanut butter would be that brown gunky stuff that sticks to the roof of your mouth. And where would printers be without designers? And vice versa. As the best in the business will

GREAT PAIRINGS

admit: Behind every great printer is a great designer, and behind every great designer is a great printer. That's the reason we have added a new Designer Awards component to the 2004 Sappi North America Printer of the Year program. A panel of nationally known designers will judge all design entries, with the top 18 winners showcased in a traveling exhibition and full-color show catalog. What's more, all 18 design winners (and a guest) will be honored at an all-expense paid gala celebration at a five-star resort this spring. But hurry, the entry deadline is January 15.

PENTAGRAM DESIGN/SF

Call for Entries

ART DIRECTOR:	DESIGNER:	CLIENT:	TOOLS:	MATERIALS:
Kit Hinrichs	Belle How	Sappi Fine Paper	Adobe Photoshop Adobe Illustrator QuarkXPress	McCoy Silk 100 lb (text) McCoy Gloss 100 lb (cover)

THE DAVE AND ALEX SHOW
The Dave and Alex Show Broadside

ART DIRECTORS	DESIGNER	CLIENT	TOOLS	MATERIALS
Alex Isley	Dana Moran	The Dave and Alex Show	QuarkXPress	Newsprint
Dave Goldenberg				

HORNALL ANDERSON DESIGN WORKS, INC.

Washington Wizards 2004 Mini Brochure

ART DIRECTOR:	DESIGNERS:	DESIGNERS:	CLIENT:	TOOLS:
Jack Anderson	Jack Anderson	Jay Hilburn	Washington Wizards	Adobe Photoshop
	Elmer dela Cruz	Beckon Wyld		QuarkXPress
	Henry Yiu	Jeff Wolff		
	Belinda Bowling	Alan Copeland		

NESNADNY + SCHWARTZ

SMART Papers Kromekote Brochure

ART DIRECTORS:	DESIGNERS:	CLIENT:	TOOLS:	MATERIALS:
Mark Schwartz	Joyce Nesnadny	SMART Papers	Adobe Photoshop	SMART Kromekote
Joyce Nesnadny	Gregory Oznowich		Adobe Illustrator	
Gregory Oznowich	Stacie Ross		QuarkXPress	

WATTS DESIGN

Spicers Paper Synthetic Paper Promotion

ART DIRECTOR:	DESIGNER:	CLIENT:	TOOLS:	MATERIALS:
Peter Watts	Peter Watts	Spicers Paper	Adobe Photoshop	Synthetic Paper range
			Adobe Illustrator	

MAGMA [BÜRO FÜR GESTALTUNG] & CHRISTIAN ERNST
VERSUS FTS_VS_PIX

ART DIRECTORS:	DESIGNERS:	TYPE DESIGN:	CLIENT:	TOOLS:
Lars Harmsen	Lars Harmsen	Boris Kahl	Volcano Type	Adobe Photoshop
Ulrich Weib	Chris Steurer	Lars Harmsen		Adobe Illustrator
Christian Ernst	Axel Brinkmann	Axel Brinkmann		Macromedia Freehand
				Macromedia Fontographer
				QuarkXPress

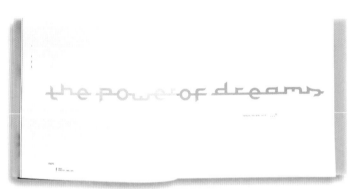

USINE DE BOUTONS

Maya Runs

ART DIRECTOR:	DESIGNERS:	CLIENT:	TOOLS:
Chiara Grandesso	Chiara Grandesso	USINE de BOUTONS	Adobe Illustrator
	Lionello Borean		

TRACY DESIGN COMMUNICATIONS
DDM Morris Photography Promotional

ART DIRECTOR:	DESIGNERS:	CLIENT:	TOOLS:
Jan Tracy	Tony Magliano	David Morris	Adobe Photoshop
	Rachel Karaca		Adobe Illustrator
			QuarkXPress

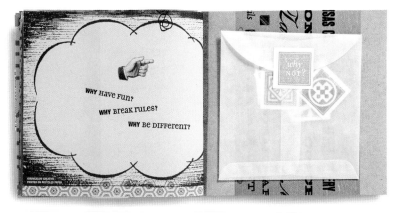

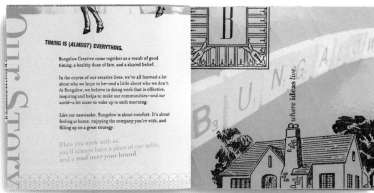

BUNGALOW CREATIVE

The Bungalow Book

ART DIRECTOR:	WRITER/EDITOR:	CLIENT:	PRINTERS:	MATERIALS:
Christopher Huelshorst	Stacey Hsu	Bungalow Creative	Hammerpress Letterpress	French Durotone
DESIGNER:	PHOTOGRAPHER:		Quality Litho	Newsprint
Christine Taylor	Jake Johnson		TOOLS:	Strathmore recycled
			Adobe Photoshop	natural white labels
			QuarkXPress	Chipboard letterpress
				scraps from Hammerpress

185

PENTAGRAM DESIGN/SF

Self-Promotion

ART DIRECTOR:	DESIGNER:	CLIENT:	TOOLS:	MATERIALS:
Kit Hinrichs	David Asari	Pentagram	Adobe Photoshop	McCoy 100 lb
			Adobe Illustrator	uncoated (cover)
			QuarkXPress	McCoy 100 lb silk (text)

186

WEYMOUTH DESIGN
Lingo 3

ART DIRECTOR:	DESIGNERS:	CLIENT:	TOOLS:	MATERIALS:
Tom Laidlaw	Robert Krivicich	Mead Coated Papers	QuarkXPress	Mead Coated Papers
	Brad Lewthwaite		Adobe Photoshop	

WEYMOUTH DESIGN, INC.

Capabilities Brochure

ART DIRECTOR:	DESIGNER:	CLIENT:	TOOLS:	MATERIALS:
Tom Laidlaw	Jonathan Grove	Dynagraf, Inc.	Adobe Photoshop Adobe Illustrator QuarkXPress	McCoy Silk matte velvet, gloss, uncoated

DOPPIO DESIGN

Self-Promotional Piece

ART DIRECTOR:
Mauro Bertolini

DESIGNERS:
Amber Kadwell
Mauro Bertolini

CLIENT:
Doppio Design

TOOLS:
Adobe Photoshop
Adobe Illustrator

MATERIALS:
Medley Satin Uncoated
100 gsm

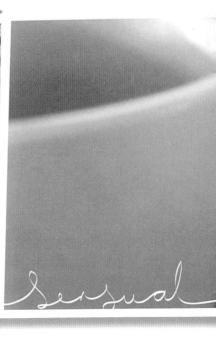

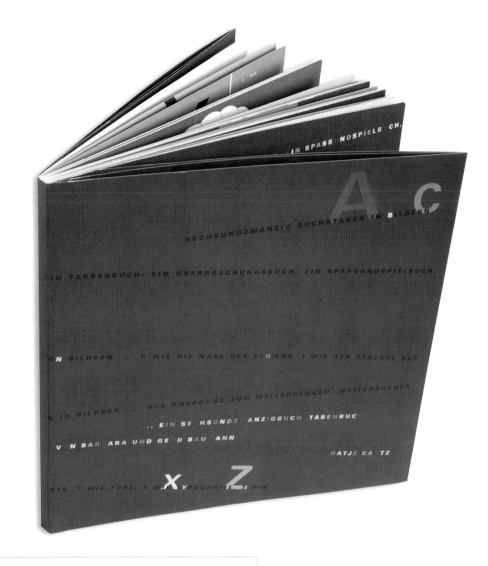

BAUMANN & BAUMANN
A Twenty-Six-Letter Book

ART DIRECTOR:	DESIGNERS:	CLIENT:	TOOLS:
Barbara Baumann	Barbara Baumann	Hatje Cantz, Ostfildern	Macromedia Freehand
Gerd Baumann	Gerd Baumann		

HIPPO STUDIO

FCS Company Brochure

ART DIRECTORS:	DESIGNERS:	CLIENT:	TOOLS:	MATERIALS:
William Ho Siu Chuen	William Ho Siu Chuen	FCS Limited	Adobe Photoshop	Curious Metallics Metal
Chin Lee Ma	Chin Lee Ma		Adobe Illustrator	Ionished Antique cover
	Stone Lam			

FLIGHT CREATIVE
Flight Creative Promotional Brochure

ART DIRECTOR:
Lisa Nankervis

DESIGNERS:
Lisa Nankervis
Alex Fregon
David Stelma

CLIENT:
Flight Creative

TOOLS:
Adobe Illustrator
3D Studio Max

MATERIALS:
Sumo 250 gsm
Central Die-cut Slit

Ó! GRAFÍSK HÖNNUN

Ó!
Self-Promotion

ART DIRECTOR:	DESIGNER:	CLIENT:	TOOLS:	MATERIALS:
Einar Gylfason	Einar Gylfason	Ó!	Macromedia Freehand	Munken Lynx

193

BLACKLETTER DESIGN INC

Self-Promotion Brochure/Book for Illustrator

ART DIRECTORS:	DESIGNER:	CLIENT:	TOOLS:	MATERIALS:
Ken Bessie	Ken Bessie	Rick Sealock	Adobe Illustrator	Stora Enso Paper Centura
Rick Sealock			QuarkXPress	

WHITE GOODS

A former Currys salesman (name and address withheld) has a few words of advice for anyone entering the High Street retail jungle in search of a new washing machine or fridge

1. Don't buy the extended warranty. Just don't.

2. Try to deal with a young man. It's a big generalisation, but a man's more likely to want to haggle with you and a young man's less likely to have mastered the art.

3. Remember that you have the power. There are at least a dozen retailers to choose from and your salesman is probably on commission.

4. If possible, go shopping without the person who'll use the machine most of the time. He or she will be much more susceptible to the salesman's silver tongue.

5. Don't be pressured into buying immediately with lines like, 'This is the last one in stock.'

6. If you're buying a fridge remember that it's about two important parts. So buy the cheaper.

7. Don't expect a big discount for cash. And if you're buying on interest-free credit, you're taking most of their margin already.

8. Reverse an old salesman's trick of tacking the extras on at the end. Agree to buy. Then say that, for example, you assume delivery is free. If he thinks he's losing a definite sale he'll soon step into line.

9. Don't be seduced by the idea that you can fit a fridge freezer into the back of your Fiat. You can't.

10. Don't buy the extended warranty.

WHITE LINES

REDPATH
The White Book

ART DIRECTORS:	DESIGNER:	CLIENT:	TOOLS:	MATERIALS:
Iain Cauder	Iain Cauder	Redpath	Adobe Illustrator	Plike 270gsm (cover)
	WRITER:		QuarkXPress	Phoenix Motion Xenou
	Paul O'Regan			170gsm (text)

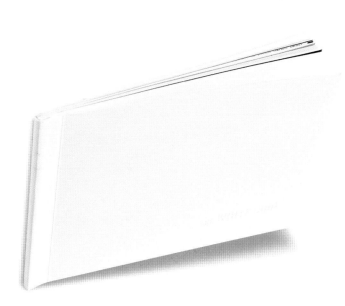

WHITE STRIPES

"We take the stars from heaven, the red from our mother country, separate it by white in stripes, thus showing we have separated from her, and the white stripes shall go down to posterity representing liberty."

George Washington

"I was looking for a quote to put in our first single that would sum up the band, and I swear to God I opened an encyclopedia at the thrift store and I opened up to the page with that quote in it. I couldn't believe it."

Jack White (guitar/vocals), The White Stripes

PENTAGRAM DESIGN, INC.

Doris Mitsch: Scanning

ART DIRECTOR:	DESIGNER:	CLIENT:	MATERIALS:
Michael Bierut	Kerrie Powell	Mohawk Paper Mills, Inc.	Mohawk Superfine Eggshell White

now here's a funny thing...

HAT-TRICK DESIGN
now here's a funny thing . . .

ART DIRECTORS:	DESIGNERS:	CLIENT:	TOOLS:	MATERIALS:
Gareth Howat	Gareth Howat	Scott Perry	QuarkXPress	Sugar Paper
David Kimpton	Jim Sutherland			
Jim Sutherland				

it's funny how things creep up

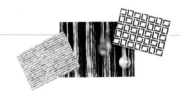

ARTS | ENTERTAINMENT
EVENTS

FUSZION GREENZWEIGDESIGN POULIN+MORRISINC ALRDESIGN DUFFY
VESTIBULESTUDIO KATSUIDESIGNOFFICE HORNALLANDERSONDESIGNWORKS ELFEN
GREENZWEIGDESIGN POULIN+MORRISINC BLUERIVERDESIGN ALRDESIGN DUFFYSINGAPORE VESTIBUL
HORNALLANDERSONDESIGNWORKS ELFEN KOLEGRAM FUSZION GREENZWEIGDES
POULIN+MORRISINC ALRDESIGN DUFFYSINGAPORE VESTIBULESTUDIO KATSUIDES
HORNALLANDERSONDESIGNWORKS GREENZWEIGDESIGN POULIN+
ALRDESIGN DUFFYSINGAPORE VESTIBULE.NET HORNALLAN
DESIGNWORKS KOLEGRAM FUSZION GREENZWEIGDESIGN POULIN+MORRISINC BLUERIVER

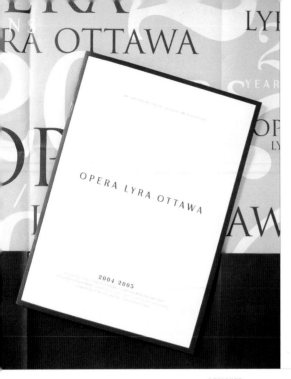

KOLEGRAM

Opera Lyra Ottawa Season Brochure

DESIGNER:
Gontran Blais

CLIENT:
Opera Lyra Ottawa

TOOLS:
Adobe Photoshop
Adobe Illustrator
QuarkXPress

MATERIALS:
Domtar Plainfield

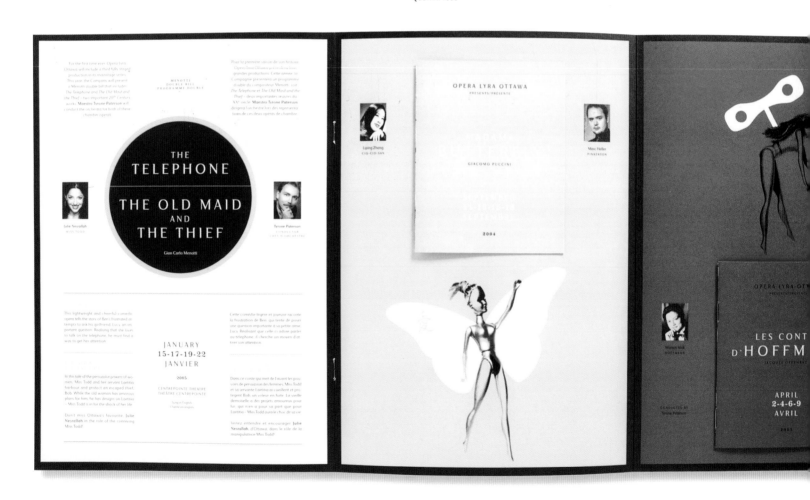

KOLEGRAM

La Chambre des Cultures Artist Catalogue

ART DIRECTOR:	DESIGNER:	CLIENT:	TOOLS:
Mike Teixeira	Mike Teixeira	Axenéo 7	Adobe Photoshop
			QuarkXPress

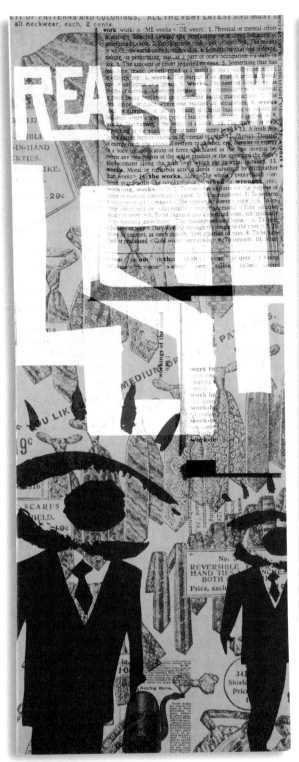

FUSZION COLLABORATIVE

Real Show Reception

ART DIRECTOR:	DESIGNER:	CLIENT:	TOOLS:	MATERIALS:
John Foster	John Foster	ADCMW	Adobe Photoshop	Domtar Titanium
			Adobe Illustrator	
			QuarkXPress	

GREENZWEIG DESIGN

Art Jam 6—Buyers Invitation

ART DIRECTOR:
Tim Greenzweig

DESIGNER:
Tim Greenzweig

CLIENT:
Graphic Artists Guild
Seattle

TOOLS:
Adobe Photoshop
QuarkXPress

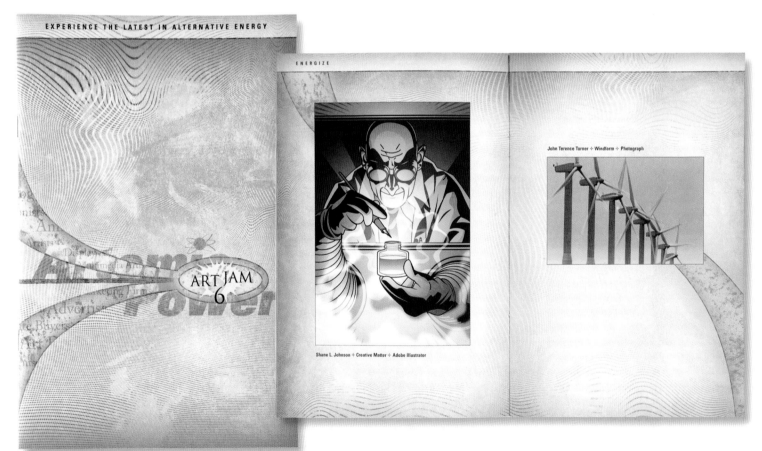

POULIN + MORRIS INC.

Dahesh Museum of Art Public Information Brochures

ART DIRECTOR:	DESIGNERS:	CLIENT:	TOOLS:	MATERIALS:
L. Richard Poulin	L. Richard Poulin	Dahesh Museum of Art	QuarkXPress	Zanders Ikono Dull Satin
	Brian Brindisi			
	Anna Crider			

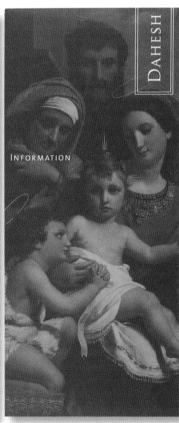

customs house gallery

BLUE RIVER DESIGN LTD.

Customs House Gallery Brochure

ART DIRECTOR:	**DESIGNER:**	**CLIENT:**	**TOOLS:**	**MATERIALS:**
Cathy Graham	Cathy Graham	Customs House Gallery	QuarkXPress	Arctic Volume 170 gsm

shoreline
where sea meets land
watery bodies
touch bone
misshapen thoughts
turn to porous stone
jagged lives
assume a form
a glass memory   a poem
and so these parts
survive the storm
and find a home

julia darling

lindsay duncanson

ALR DESIGN

These Very Serious Jokes Brochure, Joan of Arc
Brochure, 2003–2004 Season Brochure

ART DIRECTOR:
Noah Scalin

CLIENT:
Target Margin Theater

TOOLS:
Adobe Photoshop
Adobe InDesign
QuarkXPress

MATERIALS:
Process Chlorine Free
20% post-consumer
recycled paper
soy ink

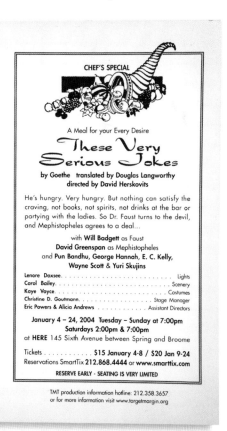

What Does The Title Mean?

"These Very Serious Jokes" is the phrase Goethe used to
describe his masterpiece, just before he died.

So Is It Goethe's *Faust*?

Yes, but only the first section. Target Margin will present
every bit of Goethe's *Faust* as a series of separate
productions spread over the next three seasons.

Tasting Menu

Before our Main Course, TMT will be presenting a series of one-
night events to whet your appetite. All Tastings will be presented
at **HERE** (see details at right). . . . . $5 each

Damn Yankees
TMT tackles a staged reading of the
Faust inspired Broadway classic.
directed by Kristin Marting
Saturday December 6 at 7pm

Bussoni's Doktor Faust
TMT performs a reading/
interpretation of the opera by this
20th century musical innovator.
directed by Donya Washington
Sunday December 7 at 7pm

UrFaust
A reading of Goethe's original
youthful version of the play.
directed by Eric Powers
Wednesday December 10 at 7pm

Kino Faust
Faust in glorious 16mm!
See how the classic tale influenced
the world of celluloid.
Sunday December 14 at 2pm

Faust Pro Musica
An evening of operatic and symphonic tidbits
based on Goethe. Performed Live!
curated by Thomas Cabaniss
Monday December 15 at 7pm

graphic design and photography: ALRdesign.com

CHEF'S SPECIAL

A Meal for your Every Desire

These Very Serious Jokes

by Goethe   translated by Douglas Langworthy
directed by David Herskovits

He's hungry. Very hungry. But nothing can satisfy the
craving, not books, not spirits, not drinks at the bar or
partying with the ladies. So Dr. Faust turns to the devil,
and Mephistopheles agrees to a deal...

with **Will Badgett** as Faust
David Greenspan as Mephistopheles
and **Pun Bandhu, George Hannah, E. C. Kelly,
Wayne Scott & Yuri Skujins**

Lenore Doxsee.	Lights
Carol Bailey.	Scenery
Kaye Voyce.	Costumes
Christine D. Goutmann.	Stage Manager
Eric Powers & Alicia Andrews	Assistant Directors

January 4 – 24, 2004 Tuesday at 7:00pm
Saturdays 2:00pm & 7:00pm
at **HERE** 145 Sixth Avenue between Spring and Broome

Tickets . . . . $15 January 4-8 / $20 Jan 9-24
Reservations SmartTix 212.868.4444 or www.smarttix.com

RESERVE EARLY - SEATING IS VERY LIMITED

TMT production information hotline: 212.358.3657
or for more information visit www.targetmargin.org

DUFFY SINGAPORE

A Programme Guide for a Play

ART DIRECTOR:	DESIGNER:	CLIENT:	TOOLS:	MATERIALS:
Christopher Lee	Kai Yeo	The Necessary Stage	Macromedia Freehand	Chipboard (cover) Woodfree (text)

DATA-BASED ART : A FULL DAY'S INVESTIGATION INTO HOW ARTISTS CREATE NEW ELECTRONIC AND DIGITAL MEDIA WORKS FROM THE MANIPULATION, PROCESSING AND ANALYSIS OF INFORMATION 18.09.03

LEV MANOVICH SOFT CINEMA
CORNELIA SOLLFRANK STEVE DIETZ
GRAHAM HARWOOD SARAH COOK
SEBASTIAN CAMPION SEMINAR
BRIAN DUFFY MODIFIED TOY ORCHESTRA
RUPERT HUBER RADIOTOPIA

SEMINAR 10.00 – 18.00, £15 (incl lunch) Level 1 Performance Space

Sessions will outline the historical context and current landscape of database-driven art projects and will feature presentations by curators, theorists, designers and artists including Cornelia Sollfrank, Steve Dietz, Graham Harwood, Sebastian Campion and Lev Manovich. Chaired by Sarah Cook.

Seminar places are limited and pre-booking is essential. Email newmedia@balticmill.com or telephone 0191 478 1810. For further information visit www.balticmill.com

WORKSHOP Brian Duffy and the Modified Toy Orchestra, Drop in between 10.00 – 18.00, Free, Level 1 Cube

Brian Duffy is a sound artist and performer based in Birmingham. His work includes record production, installations, live performances and the creation of 'surplus value objects', often from old electronic toys. Bring your own electronic sound toys and work with Brian to rewire and reconfigure them to create new musical instruments. For further information on this workshop email newmedia@balticmill.com

No pre-booking required.

EXHIBITION Lev Manovich, Soft Cinema 10.00 – 22.00, Free, Level 1 Orientation Space

Lev Manovich is a digital media artist and theorist currently in residence at BALTIC. Soft Cinema is an ambient cinema project that uses a large database to generate short narrative films. Come and see the latest developments in this dynamic multimedia artwork. www.manovich.net/softcinema2

No pre-booking required.

LIVE PERFORMANCE Rupert Huber: Radiotopia 20.00 – 22.00, Free, Level 1 Performance Space

Rupert Huber is a composer and musician based in Vienna who uses a digital filesharing system to create electronic sound performances. The database is divided into three parts: input, transformation and output. Sounds can be sent into the database, mixed and changed there, and taken out of the database for local broadcasting use. Using both his own archive of completed compositions and the Radiotopia database of archived sounds, Rupert Huber will live mix and seamlessly transition between solo work and collaborative work in his performance, incorporating sounds generated by Brian Duffy and the Modified Toy Orchestra.

No pre-booking required.

BALTIC

BALTIC The Centre for Contemporary Art
South Shore Road, Gateshead
NE8 3BA England
info@balticmill.com www.balticmill.com
Tel: +44 (0)191 478 1810
Fax: +44 (0)191 478 1922

Gallery opening hours: Mon, Tues, Wed, Fri,
Sat 10:00 - 19:00 Thurs 10:00 - 22:00, Sun
10:00 - 17:00 Free Admission

BALTIC is funded by the National Lottery through
Arts Council England, Gateshead Council, European
Regional Development Fund, One NorthEast

These events have been organised by BALTIC in partnership with CRUMB
at the University of Sunderland. With support from Arts Council England.

Cover Image: Lev Manovich, Soft Cinema database

BLUE RIVER DESIGN LTD.

Baltic Seminar Leaflet, M&S Lifestone Leaflet, Baltic Hiller Invitation

ART DIRECTOR:	DESIGNERS:	CLIENT:	TOOLS:	MATERIALS:
Lisa Thundercliffe	Lisa Thundercliffe	Baltic Contemporary	Macromedia Freehand	Challenger offset 70 gsm
Cathy Graham	Cathy Graham	Arts Centre	QuarkXPress	Sovereign Silk 170 gsm
James Askham	James Askham			

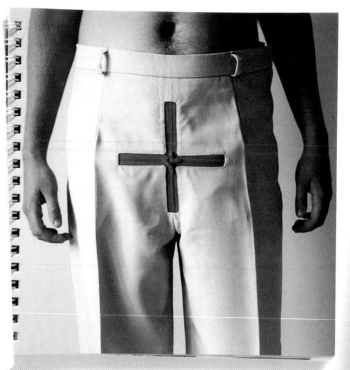

ELEMENT

CSCA Call For Entries

ART DIRECTOR:	DESIGNER:	CLIENT:	TOOLS:	MATERIALS:
Jeremy Slagle	Jeremy Slagle	Columbus Society of Community Arts	Adobe InDesign Macromedia Freehand	Scheufelen Phoenix Motion White

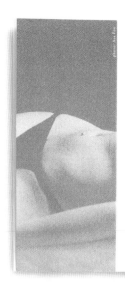

Please be my guest at my most recent production of

The Blue Room
by David Hare

Freely adapted from Arthur Schnitzler's *La Ronde*

Regional Premiere
The Hangar Theatre
Ithaca, NY

June 18–26, 2004

www.hangartheatre.org

Daring, dramatic, and highly theatrical, The Blue Room explores the treacherous disparity between longing and love, passion and intimacy. In a sequence of dialogues, two actors play ten couples, linked one to the other by the most universal of human desires.

Girl meets boy, meets girl, meets boy...

"[The Blue Room] provides a sad, wise, unflinchingly honest view of human nature."
The Daily Telegraph

"[Schnitzler's] essential subject is the gulf between what we imagine, what we remember, and what we actually experience."
David Hare

Wendy Dann
director

Greetings!

You've received several copies of my resume, and now it's time to see some of my work. The Blue Room runs for two weeks this June, and I'd love for you to be my guest at one of the performances.

You may have seen some of my previous work: I currently serve as Associate Artistic Director at the Hangar Theatre, and directed *Stones in His Pockets* for the Hangar season in 2003. Selected directing credits include *Chesapeake* at Syracuse Stage; *Dancing at Lughnasa* at the Cider Mill Playhouse; *Nora, The Unexpected Man, Three Days of Rain, Chesapeake, The Soup Comes Last, The Cripple of Inishmaan* at the Kitchen Theatre Company; and *Translations, Wit, The Beauty Queen of Leenane,* and *Hamlet* at Syracuse University. I enjoyed a spring as the Directing Fellow at the GEVA Theatre Center in Rochester. I have also taught acting and directing at Ithaca College, Syracuse University, and Cornell University.

My full resume and production photos are available at www.wendydann.com

I look forward to seeing you in The Blue Room.

Wendy Dann
313 Columbia Street
Ithaca, NY 14850

postcard photo by Ashley Delleferer

Please reserve one/two (please circle) tickets
under my name for the following performance:

___ Friday, June 18 at 8pm
___ Saturday, June 19 at 3pm
___ Saturday, June 19 at 8pm
___ Sunday, June 20 at 7:30 pm
___ Tuesday, June 22 at 7:30 pm
___ Wednesday, June 23 at 7:30pm
___ Thursday, June 24 at 7:30 pm
___ Friday, June 25 at 8pm
___ Saturday, June 26 at 3pm
___ Saturday, June 26 at 8 pm

Name:
Phone:

Your tickets will be at the will call window
at the theatre on the evening of performance.

THE HUMAN RACE

Theatrical Invitation

ART DIRECTOR:	DESIGNERS:	CLIENT:	TOOLS:	MATERIALS:
Xanthe Matychak	Xanthe Matychak	Wendy Dann, Theatrical Director	Adobe Photoshop Adobe Illustrator	1 Color Uncoated Stock

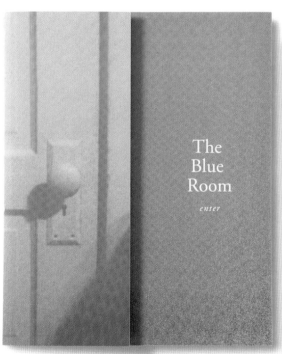

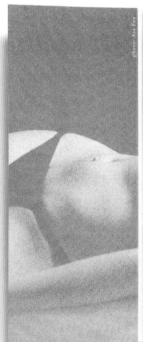

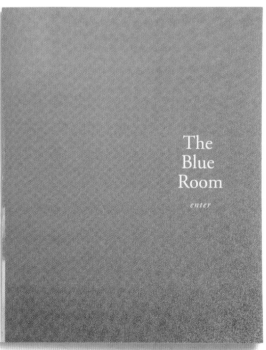

The Blue Room *enter*

The Blue Room *enter*

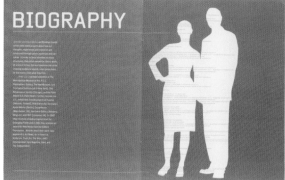

VESTIBULE STUDIO

Robot Films Catalogue

ART DIRECTORS:	DESIGNERS:	CLIENT:	TOOLS:
Suzan Ting	Suzan Ting	Fact Foundation for Arts	Adobe Photoshop
Bruno Ricard	Bruno Ricard	& Creative Tech	Adobe Illustrator
			QuarkXPress

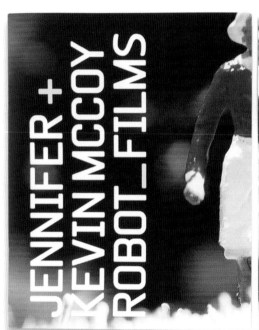

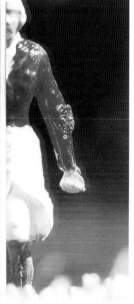

KATSUI DESIGN OFFICE INC.

Tategumi Yokogumi Morisawa Quarterly 2002, No. 57

ART DIRECTOR:
Mitsuo Katsui

DESIGNERS:
Mitsuo Katsui
Takeo Nakano

CLIENT:
Morisaw & Company Ltd.

TOOLS:
Adobe Photoshop
Adobe Illustrator

MATERIALS:
Fancy papers

HORNALL ANDERSON DESIGN WORKS, INC.

Seattle Super Sonics 2004 Brochure

ART DIRECTOR:
Jack Anderson

DESIGNERS:
Jack Anderson
Andrew Wicklund

CLIENT:
Seattle SuperSonics

ELFEN

Craft Catalogue

ART DIRECTOR:	DESIGNER:	CLIENT:	TOOLS:	MATERIALS:
Guto Evans	Matthew James	Wales Arts International	Macromedia Freehand QuarkXPress	Curtis Echo Artik matt

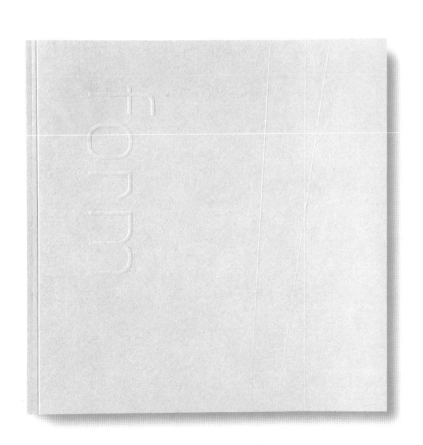

THE RUSSO-JAPANESE WAR

During the Russo-Japanese War (1904–5), more than one million Japanese soldiers fought Russian troops for control of Korea and Manchuria. Postcards—which from the beginning had been used for documentation, memorialization, and propaganda—were particularly relevant in wartime and became the preferred way for families to maintain contact with the armed forces and follow the progress of the war. The Japanese government issued five sets of postcards with scenes of battles, courageous soldiers, and victory celebrations. The demand for these was so great that between 400,000 and 700,000 sets were printed in Tokyo alone.

Among the privately printed postcards are ones extending across three cards, with a striking Russian ship juxtaposed against a stylized map of Japan (fig. 2). The inscription along the bottom edge notes that the cards were designed for a competition, presumably in commemoration of Japan's victory.

individual cards were issued. In addition, approximately one thousand sets of privately printed postcards (forty-five hundred different designs) fed the frenzy, and by the time the war was over, an estimated four thousand postcard outlets existed in Tokyo alone.

On June 1, 1906, the government issued its last set of postcards, celebrating the Japanese victory. This set included a photographic image documenting thousands of people waiting in line to buy these postcards (see page 15, fig. 12). At top and lower right of the card are lithographs showing customers completing their purchases and an official providing commemorative stamps. One observer noted: "When unsuccessful buyers were given a notice that all cards had gone, they stoned the office and smashed window panes."

fig. 2
Commemorating the Great Naval Battle of the Japan Sea (detail), late Meiji era, canceled 1906

NEW YEAR'S POSTCARDS

fig. 9
Takahashi Haruka (dates unknown), New Year's Card: Goat, Shōwa era, 1931

Atsuo (dates unknown), New Year's Card: Women in Au Courant Fashion with Cityscape, Taishō–early Shōwa eras
fig. 10

The exchange of greetings at New Year's—traditionally in the form of personal visits—has been a revered custom in Japan since ancient times. When the mail system was established, however, the increasingly popular postcard became the favorite way to send good wishes to friends and relatives. It has been estimated that in 1905, for example, more than one hundred million postcards were sent to commemorate the New Year.

Many New Year's cards feature the twelve animals of the East Asian zodiac, which originated in China but has been known in Japan for almost two thousand years. The animals are placed in a traditional order to count the years. The years of the goat (fig. 9), for example, are 1907, 1919, 1931, and so on, up to 2003.

ART OF THE JAPANESE POSTCARD
THE LEONARD A. LAUDER COLLECTION AT THE MFA, BOSTON

MUSEUM OF FINE ARTS, BOSTON
Japanese Postcard Exhibit Brochure

ART DIRECTOR:	DESIGNER:	CLIENT:	TOOLS:	MATERIALS:
Janet O'Donoghue	Melissa Wehrman	Museum of Fine Arts Boston	Adobe Photoshop QuarkXPress	Monadnock Astrolite Silk Text 100 lb

POSTCARDS AS ADVERTISEMENTS

Early Japanese advertising postcards primarily featured photographs, but designers soon enriched these photographs with bold, swirling borders influenced by Art Nouveau. After 1914, advertising design entered a new era, in which many styles of modern art were employed by artists who decided to become graphic designers rather than painters (fig. 7). Due to mechanical forms of reproduction and an increasing reliance of technology, graphic design—which created multiples for mass consumption rather than unique objects for the individual—became a field in its own right.

Sugiura Hisui was a central figure in gaining recognition for graphic design as

fig. 7
Commemorating the Ninth Tournament of Far Eastern Athletes, early Shōwa era, 1930

a legitimate artistic pursuit. Working in an eclectic, East/West style, Hisui produced posters, brochures, magazine illustrations, and postcards for a number of companies, including the department store Mitsukoshi (fig. 8).

Founded as a dry-goods store in central Edo, Mitsukoshi (still operating today) flourished with Japan's economy and soon had branches throughout the country and elsewhere in Asia, hiring consultants who had studied American department store management. Mitsukoshi introduced glass display cases and show windows, and installed the country's first escalator in its main store. Mitsukoshi ultimately hired western architecture, a job previously held only by men in Japan. In another radical departure from tradition, the store no longer required shoppers to leave their shoes at the entrance of the store.

fig. 8
Sugiura Hisui (1876–1965), Commemorating the New Building of Mitsukoshi Department Store in Osaka, late Meiji era

MIRKO ILIĆ CORP.

B/W Zagreb

ART DIRECTOR:	DESIGNER:	CLIENT:	TOOLS:
Mirko Ilić	Mirko Ilić	SLM	QuarkXPress

works/san josé

the first quarter-century

JOE MILLER'S COMPANY

Works 25th-Anniversary Catalog

DESIGNER:	CLIENT:	TOOLS:	MATERIALS:
Joe Miller	Works/San Jose	Adobe Photoshop	Crushed Leaf Sparkles
		Adobe Illustrator	(cover)
		QuarkXPress	Crushed Leaf (text)
			Sandstone (text)
			Cougar Opaque White
			(text)

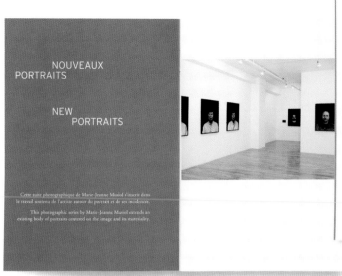

NOUVEAUX
PORTRAITS

NEW
PORTRAITS

Cette suite photographique de Marie-Jeanne Musiol s'inscrit dans
le travail soutenu de l'artiste autour du portrait et de ses incidences.

This photographic series by Marie-Jeanne Musiol extends an
existing body of portraits centered on the image and its materiality.

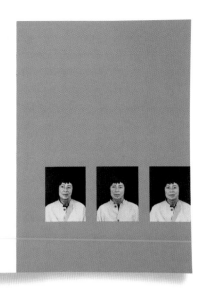

KOLEGRAM

Art Exhibit Brochure

ART DIRECTOR:
Mike Teixeira

DESIGNER:
Mike Teixeira

CLIENT:
Pierre-François Ouellette
Art Contemporain

TOOLS:
Adobe Photoshop
QuarkXPress

MATERIALS:
Potlach McCoy

Marie-Jeanne Musiol

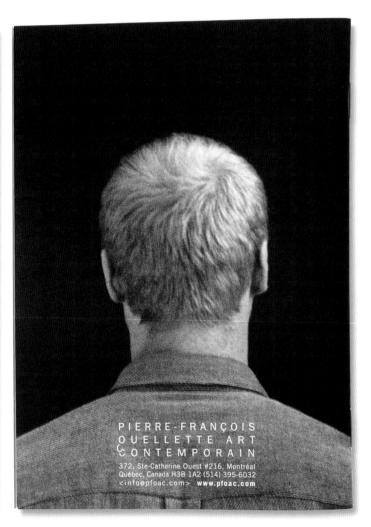

PIERRE-FRANÇOIS
OUELLETTE ART
CONTEMPORAIN
372, Ste-Catherine Ouest #216, Montréal
Québec, Canada H3B 1A2 (514) 395-6032
<info@pfoac.com> www.pfoac.com

207 **ALR DESIGN**
2701 Edgewood Avenue
Richmond, VA 23222
United States
phone/fax: 804.321.6677
contact@ALRdesign.com

117 **ALTERPOP**
128 1001 Mariposa Street #304
San Francisco, CA 94122
United States
phone: 415.558.1515
fax: 415.558.8422
mail@alterpop.com

115 **AND PARTNERS**
156 Fifth Avenue #1234
New York, NY 10010
United States
phone: 212.414.4700
fax: 212.414.2915
david@andpartnersny.com

86 **ANTFARM INC**
89 132 East 10th Street
St. Paul, MN 55101
United States
phone: 612.362.0000
fax: 651.298.9777
dbehrens@antfarminc.com

98 **BAILEY/FRANKLIN**
0121 Southwest Bancroft Street
Portland, OR 97239-4051
United States
phone: 503.228.1381
fax: 503.228.9173
connie@baileyfranklin.com

62 **BAKKEN CREATIVE CO.**
1250 Addison Street #206
Berkeley, CA 94702
United States
phone: 510.540.8260
fax: 510.540.8269
mbakken@bakkencreativeco.com

16 **BANDUJO DONKER & BROTHERS**
17 22 West 19th Street, 9th Floor
26 New York, NY 10011
United States
phone: 212.322.4100
fax: 212.366.6068
jbandujo@bandujo.com

22 **BAUMANN & BAUMANN**
190 Taubentalstrabe 4/1
73525 Schwabisch Gmund
Germany
phone: 49.7171.927990
fax: 49.7171.927999
info@baumannandbaumann.com

32 **BBK STUDIO**
151 648 Monroe Northwest, Suite 212
Grand Rapids, MI 49503
United States
phone: 616.459.4444
fax: 616.459.4477
yang@bbkstudio.com

30 **BERTZ DESIGN GROUP**
190 Washington Street
Middletown, CT 06457
United States
phone: 860.347.4332
fax: 860.347.1008
max@bertzdesign.com

194 **BLACKLETTER DESIGN INC.**
#391 Regal Park Northeast
Calgary, AB T2E 056 Canada
phone/fax: 403.276.5428
sealock@telusplanet.net

206 **BLUE RIVER DESIGN LTD.**
209 The Foundry, Forth Banks
Newcastle upon Tyne, England NE1 3PA
United Kingdom
phone: 44.0191.261.0000
fax: 44.0191.261.0010
design@blueriverdesign.co.uk

31 **BNIM ARCHITECTS**
147 106 West 14th Street, Suite 200
163 Kansas City, MO 64105
United States
phone: 816.783.1500
fax: 816.783.1501
egehle@bnim.com

71 **BRUKETA & ZINIC**
Zavrtnica 17
Zagreb, 10000
Croatia
phone: 385.16064.000
fax: 385.16064.001
bruketa-zinic@ bruketa-zinic.com

185 **BUNGALOW CREATIVE**
1911 Wyandotte
Kansas City, MO 64108
United States
phone: 816.914.6621
christopher@bungalowcreative.com

19 **BURGARD DESIGN GROUP**
342 Walnut Street
Columbia, PA 17512
United States
phone/fax: 717.684.5896
gideon@redrose.net

103 **CACAO DESIGN**
C.so San Gouardo 18
20136 Milano, Italy
phone: 39.02.8942.2896
fax: 39.02.5810.6789
mauro@cacaodesign.it

43 **CARBONE SMOLAN AGENCY**
22 West 19th Street, 10th Floor
New York, NY 10011-4204
United States
phone: 212.807.0011
fax: 212.807.0870
lynn@carbonesmolan.com

157 **CDT DESIGN**
21 Brownlow Mews
London, England WCIN 2LG
United Kingdom
phone: 44.207.242.0992
fax: 44.207.242.1174
tania@cdt-design.co.uk

70 **CF NAPA**
1130 Main Street
Napa, CA 94559
United States
phone: 707.265.1891
fax: 707.265.1899
dschuemann@cfnapa.com

120 **CONCRETE**
407 South Dearborn Street, Suite 230
Chicago, IL 60605
United States
phone: 312.427.3733
fax: 312.427.9053
jilly@concrete-us.com

135 **DANIELLE FOUSHÉE DESIGN**
1373 North 310 West #2
Logan, UT 84341
United States
phone: 818.613.7459
danielle@daniellefoushee.com

134 **ANNE-LISE DERMENGHEM**
7, rue Édouard Nortier
Neuilly-sur-Seine 92200
France
phone | fax: 33.1.47.38.24.05
lacblanc@hotmail.com

12 **THE DAVE AND ALEX SHOW**
178 9 Brookside Place
Redding, CT 06896
United States
phone: 203.544.7137
fax: 203.544.7189
aline@daveandalex.com

158 **DESIGN AHEAD**
Ruschenstrasse 18
Essen, D-45133
Germany
phone: 49.201.84.2060
voss@design-ahead.com

189 **DOPPIO DESIGN**
Studio 7, 13-15 Smail Street, Ultimo
Sydney, NSW, Australia 2007
phone: 61.2.9212.0405
fax: 61.2.6280.2457
studio@doppiodesign.com

162 **DUFFY SINGAPORE**
208 25 Duxton Hill
Singapore 089608
phone: 65.6324.7827
fax: 65.6324.8265
michelle.tan@fallon.com

13 **EAT ADVERTISING & DESIGN, INC.**
2 West 39th, Suite 204
Kansas City, MO 64111
United States
phone: 816.931.2687
fax: 816.931.0723
patrice@eatinc.com

215 **ELFEN**
20 Harrowby Lane
Cardiff Bay, Cardiff, Wales
United Kingdom
phone: 44.0.292.048.4824
guto@elfen.co.uk

66 **ELEMENT**
210 3292-C North High Street
Columbus, OH 43202
United States
phone: 614.447.0406
fax: 614.447.1417
jeremy@elementville.com

28 **EQUUS DESIGN CONSULTANTS PTE LTD**
60 8B Murray Terrace
Singapore 079522
phone: 65.6323.2996
fax: 65.6323.2991
muisan@equus-design.com

192 **FLIGHT CREATIVE**
Studio 14/15 Inkerman Street
St. Kilda, Victoria 3182
Australia
phone: 61.3.9534.4690
fax: 61.3.9593.6029
mail@flightcreative.com.au

203 **FUSZION COLLABORATIVE**
225 North Fairfax Street, 2nd Floor
Alexandria, VA 22314
United States
phone: 703.548.8080
fax: 703.548.8382
john@fuszion.com

10 **GEE + CHUNG DESIGN**
38 Bryant Street, Suite 100
San Francisco, CA 94105
United States
phone: 415.543.1192
fax: 415.543.6088
earl@geechungdesign.com

121 **GEORGE TSCHERNY, INC.**
238 East 72 Street
New York, NY 10021
United States
phone: 212.734.3277
fax: 212.734.3278
gtscherny@aol.com

14 **GRAFIKZ**
42 Pamplona, 33 Casa 3
Sao Paulo, Spain 01405.000
phone: 34.55.11.3171.2153
apolessi@grafikz.com

74 **GRAPHICULTURE**
93 322 1st Avenue North #500
Minneapolis, MN 55401
United States
phone: 612.339.8271
fax: 612.339.1436
janice.stanford@graphiculture.com

204 **GREENZWEIG DESIGN**
13546 36th Avenue Northeast
Seattle, WA 98125
United States
phone: 206.890.0972
fax: 206.417.1821
tim@greenzweig.com

149 **GRETEMAN GROUP**
1425 East Douglas, Suite 200
Wichita, KS 67211
United States
phone: 316.263.1004
fax: 316.263.1060
sgreteman@gretemangroup.com

27 **HALLMARK CARDS, INC.**
2501 McGee
Kansas City, MO 64108
United States
phone: 816.274.5727
ctaylo2@halimark.com

141 **HAMMERPRESS**
1919 Wyandotte
Kansas City, MO 64108
United States
phone: 816.421.1929
brady@hammerpress.net

24 **HANGAR 18 CREATIVE GROUP**
152 Suite 220, 1737 West Third Avenue
Vancouver, BC V6J 1K7
Canada
phone: 603.737.7111
fax: 604.737.7166
sean@hangar18.bc.ca

34 **HAT-TRICK DESIGN**
82 3rd Floor 3 Morocco Street
122 London, England SE1 3HB
197 United Kingdom
phone: 44.020.7403.7875
fax: 44.020.7403.8926
adam@hat-trickdesign.co.uk

105 **HIPPO STUDIO**
191 Room 2C Queen's Centre
58 Queen's Road East
Wanchai, Hong Kong
phone: 852.2529.6700
fax: 852.2529.9269
design@hippostudio.com

55 **HORNALL ANDERSON DESIGN WORKS**
67 1008 Western Avenue, Suite 600
69 Seattle, WA 98104
76 United States
179 phone: 206.826.2329
214 fax: 206.467.6411
c_arbini@hadw.com

44 **HOWRY DESIGN ASSOCIATES**
45 354 Pine Street #600
54 San Francisco, CA 94104
United States
phone: 415.433.2035
fax: 415.433.0816
bill@howry.com

150 **RUTH HUIMERIND**
Rannaku PST 9-29
Tallinn 10917, Estonia
phone: 372.6777243
fax: 372.6276771
rosa.permanente@mail.ee

91 **IMAGINE**
The Stables, Paradise Wharf
Ducie Street, Manchester, England
United Kingdom M1 2JN
phone: 44.0.161.272.8334
david@miagine-cga.co.uk

51 **IMELDA AGENCY**
Reslyeva 35
Lyublyana-Slovenijaeu
phone: 386.01.434.7348
stvarnik.doo@siol.net

79 **INARIA**
95 Power Road Studios:
132 114 Power Road
London, England W45 PY
United Kingdom
phone: 44.0.20.8996.5736
fax: 44.0.20.8996.5739
debora@inaria-design.com

164 **INSIGHT DESIGN COMMUNICATIONS**
322 South Mosley
Wichita, KS 67202
United States
phone: 316.262.0085
fax: 316.264.5420
tracy@idcweb.net

156 **IRON DESIGN**
120 North Aurora Street
Ithaca, NY 14850
United States
phone: 607.275.9544
fax: 607.275.0370
todd@irondesign.com

65 **JASON & JASON**
11B Hayetzira Street
Post Office Box 2432
Ra'anana 43663
Israel
phone: 972.9.7444282
fax: 972.9.7444292
tamar@jasonandjason.com

218 **JOE MILLER'S COMPANY**
3080 Olcott Street, Suite 210A
Santa Clara, CA 95054
United States
phone: 408.988.2924
joecompany@aol.com

213 **KATSUI DESIGN OFFICE INC.**
3-48-9 nishihara
Shibuya-ku, Tokyo 151-0066 Japan
phone: 81.3.5478.7681
fax: 81.3.5478.8722
kdo-001@fd.catv.ne.jp

171 **KBDA**
2558 Overland Avenue
Los Angeles, CA 90064
United States
phone: 310.287.2400
fax: 310.287.0909
kim@kbda.com

AGENCY DIRECTORY

169 KOLEGRAM
200 37. Boulevard St. Joseph
202 Hull, Quebec, Canada
219 phone: 819.777.5538
fax: 819.777.8525
gblais@kolegram.com

175 LIQUID AGENCY INC.
448 South Market Street
San Jose, CA 95113
United States
phone: 408.850.8836
fax: 408.850.8825
vincent@liquidagency.com

108 LISKA + ASSOCIATES, INC.
515 North State Street, 23rd Floor
Chicago, IL 60610
United States
phone: 312.644.4400
fax: 312.644.9650
agray@liska.com

107 LLOYDS GRAPHIC DESIGN LTD
17 Westhaven Place
Blenheim, New Zealand
phone/fax: 64.3.578.6955
lloydgraphics@xtra.co.nz

167 LOGOSBRANDS
201-81 The East Mall
Toronto, ON M8Z 5W3
Canada
phone: 416.259.7834
fax: 416.259.4053
john.miziolek@logosbrands.com

182 MAGMA [BÜRO FÜR GESTALTUNG]
Bachstrasse 43
Karlsruhe, Germany
phone: 49.721.9291970
fax: 49.721.9291980
harmsen@magma-ka.ge

83 MARIUS FAHRNER DESIGN
87 Suttnerstrasse 8
92 22765 Hamburg, Germany
phone: 49.40.43.27.1234
marius@formgefrehl.de

138 MIRKO ILIĆ CORP
217 207 East 32nd Street
New York, NY 10016
United States
phone: 212.481.9737
fax: 212.481.7088
studio@mirkoilic.com

109 MODELHART GRAFIK-DESIGN
Ing-Ludwig-Pech-Strasse 1
St. Johann, Pg, Austria 5600
phone/fax: 43.6412.4679
design@modelhart.at

50 MONSTER DESIGN
7826 Leary Way Northeast #200
Redmond, WA 98052
United States
phone: 425.828.7853
fax: 425.576.8055
info@monsterinvasion.com

140 MUSEUM OF FINE ARTS, BOSTON
216 465 Huntington Avenue
Boston, MA 02115
United States
phone: 617.369.3437
jshulman@mfa.org

129 NASSAR DESIGN
11 Park Street
Brookline, MA 02446
United States
phone: 617.264.2862
fax: 617.264.2861
n.nassar@verizon.net

123 NESNADNY + SCHWARTZ
130 10803 Magnolia Drive
170 Cleveland, OH 44106
180 United States
phone: 216.791.7721
fax: 216.791.9560
info@NSideas.com

85 NO.PARKING
88 Contrà S. Barbara, 19
101 Vincenza, Italy 36100
104 phone: 39.0444.327861
fax: 39.0444.327595
inbox@noparking.it

193 Ó!
Holtsgata 19
Reykjavik/101/Iceland
phone: 354.840.0220
fax: 354.555.4048
einar@oid.is

72 SALVA O'RENICK
511 Delaware, Suite 1
Kansas City, MO 64105
United States
phone: 816.842.6996
fax: 816.842.6989
mpaoletti@uncommonsense.com

146 PAULA KELLY DESIGN
176 42 Bank Street
New York, NY 10014
United States
phone: 212.741.5025
paulakellydesign@mindspring.com

18, 20 PENTAGRAM DESIGN/SF
25, 68 387 Tehama Street
75, 96 San Francisco, CA 94103
102 United States
177 phone: 415.896.0499
186 fax: 415.541.9106
lawson@sf.pentagram.com

196 PENTAGRAM DESIGN, INC.
204 Fifth Avenue
New York, NY 10010
United States
phone: 212.683.7000
fax: 212.532.0181
powell@pentagram.com

47 PERKS DESIGN PARTNERS
90 2nd Floor, 333 Flinders Lane
133 Melbourne, Victoria 3000
154 Australia
phone: 61.3.9620.5911
fax: 61.3.9620.5922
d.ohehir@perksdesignpartners.com

33 THE POINT GROUP
77 5949 Sherry Lane #1800
81 Dallas, TX 75225
United States
phone: 214.378.7970
fax: 214.378.7967
dhoward@thepointgroup.com

100 POMME STUDIO
65 Aberdeen Street
Quebec, Quebec G1R 2C6
Canada
phone: 418.522.1487
fax: 418.948.8988
pamela@pommestudio.com

52 POPCORN INITIATIVE
3124 Corrinne Drive
Orlando, FL 32803
United States
phone: 407.228.6601
fax: 407.228.9803
chris@popcorninitiative.com

205 POULIN + MORRIS INC.
286 Spring Street, 6th Floor
New York, NY 10013
United States
phone: 212.675.1332
fax: 212.675.3027
richard@poulinmorris.com

118 RCDP
30 Schroder Street,
Roosevelt Park
Johannesburg, 2095,
South Africa
phone: 27.11.888.5302
fax: 27.11.408.3988
brian@mindset.co.za

124 REDPATH
195 5 Gayfield Square
Edinburgh, Scotland EH1 3NW
United Kingdom
phone: 0.131.556.9115
fax: 0.131.556.9116
allison@redpath.co.uk

64 ROYCROFT DESIGN
31A Main Street
Charlestown, MA 02129
United States
phone: 617.242.4505
fax: 617.242.4501
roycroft@roycroftdesign.com

127 RUTGERS UNIVERSITY
96 Davidson Road
Piscataway, NJ 08854-8062
United States
phone: 732.445.3710
fax: 732.445.1906
jvancle@ur.rutgers.edu

15 SALTERBAXTER
39 8 Telford Road
41 London W10 5SH
48 United Kingdom
49 phone: 44.020.7401.9401
fax: 44.020.7401.8101
info@salterbaxter.com

161 SAGMEISTER INC.
222 W 14th Street, Suite 15A
New York, NY 10011
United States
phone: 212.647.1789
fax: 212.647.1788
info@sagmeister.com

106 SAVAS CEKIC DESIGN OFFICE
Havyar Sk. 27/3 Cihangir/Beyoglu
Istanbul 80060 Turkey
phone: 90.212.249.6918
fax: 90.212.245.5009
savas@savascekic.com

99 SOPHIE BARTHO + ASSOCIATES
155 285 Liverpool Street
Darlinghurst, NSW 2010
Australia
phone: 61.2.9360.5226
fax: 61.2.9360.5227
michele@bartho.com.au

136 STORM VISUAL COMMUNICATIONS INC.
137 210 Dalhousie Street
Ottawa, ON K1N 7C8
Canada
phone: 613.789.0244
fax: 613.789.0265
studio@storm.on.ca

80 TANAGRAM PARTNERS
855 West Blackhawk
Chicago, IL 60622
United States
phone: 312.787.6831
gdavis@tanagram.com

211 THE HUMAN RACE
429 North Geneva Street
Itaca, NY 14850
United States
phone: 617.273.8147
ehtnax@yahoo.com

116 TOMATO KOSIR
148 Britof 141
Kranj, Slovenia SI-4000
phone: 386.41260.979
tomato@siol.net

94 TRACY DESIGN COMMUNICATIONS
153 118 Southwest Blvd, Suite 200
165 Kansas City, MO 64108
184 United States
phone: 816.421.0606
fax: 816.421.0177
jan@tracydesign.com

84 USINE DE BOUTONS
111 Via G. Franco, 99B
144 Cadoneghe (PD), Italy 35010
159 phone: 39.049.8870953
183 fax: 39.049.8879520
hello@usine.it

212 VESTIBULE STUDIO
103 North 3rd Street
Brooklyn, NY 11211
United States
phone: 718.782.3495
fax: 718.782.5127
emailus@vestibule.net

166 VINE360
7701 France Ave S, Suite 200
Edina, MN 55435
United States
phone: 952.893.0504
fax: 952.893.0034
info@vine360.com

63 VOICE
126 217 Gilbert Street
Adelaide, South Australia 5000
phone: 61.8.8.410.8822
fax: 61.8.8.410.8933
anthony@voicedesign.net

168 WAECHTER & WAECHTER
WORLDWIDE PARTNERS
Grimmstrasse 3
80336 Munich, Germany
phone: 49.0.89.174.7242.34
fax: 49.0.89.174.7242.60
k.lange@waechter-waechter.de

119 WATTS DESIGN
181 66 Albert Road
South Melbourne, Victoria 3205
Australia
phone: 61.3.9696.4116
fax: 61.3.9696.4006
peter@wattsdesign.com.au

139 MELISSA WEHRMAN
282 Newbury Street #15
Boston, MA 02116
United States
phone: 617.247.8136
fax: 617.369.3191
melissa@melissawehrman.com

40, 46 WEYMOUTH DESIGN
53, 56 332 Congress Street
73, 172 Boston, MA 02210
187 United States
188 phone: 617.542.2647
fax: 617.451.6233
arvi@weymouthdesign.com

WILLOUGHBY DESIGN GROUP
602 Westport Road
Kansas City, MO 64111
United States
phone: 816.561.4189
fax: 816.561.5052
info@willoughbydesign.com

174 ZIGZAG DESIGN
6432 Oak Street
Kansas City, MO 64113
United States
phone: 816.213.1198
fax: 816.444.0213
info@zigzag.com

21 ZUCCHINI DESIGN PTE LTD
30A Mosque Street
Singapore 059508
phone: 65.6887.5746
fax: 65.6223.8070
sunne@zucchini.com.sg

AGENCY DIRECTORY

Ann Willoughby is the Founder and Chief Creative Officer of **Willoughby Design Group**, a brand strategy and identity design firm started in 1978. The firm specializes in integrated brand identity, communications and product design in the retail, fashion, dining, and entertainment industries.

Clients include Three Dog Bakery, Einstein Bros Bagels, Noodles and Company, Lee Jeans, Hallmark, Buckle, IBC, Playtex, and a new start-up restaurant concept, SPIN.

Willoughby's approach to design and business is reflected in the company's unique studio environment—a collaborative space where designers work alongside entrepreneurs and CEOs to visualize new retail concepts. The office, complete with a meditation room and the off-site Willoughby Design Barn retreat helps attract and retain top creative talent and brings forward-thinking clients to Kansas City.

Ann serves as a Director on the AIGA National Board. She was the Chair for the 2004 National AIGA Gain Conference in New York. Ann also serves on the national AIGA Brand Experience Board and is a member of the editorial board of *HOW*.

WILLOUGHBY DESIGN GROUP OFFICE

WILLOUGHBY DESIGN BARN

DESIGN TEAM	JUDGING TEAM	
Ann Willoughby	Ann Willoughby	Hannah Stubblefield
Anne Simmons	Becky Harbrecht	Nate Hardin
Deb Tagtalianidis	Cathy Kouris	Nicole Satterwhite
Paul Lefebvre	Chanda Fanolio	Ryan Jones
Ryan Jones	Deb Tagtalianidis	Stephanie Lee

ABOUT THE AUTHOR